American Birding Association

Field Guide to Birds of Hawai'i

Helen and André F. Raine

PHOTOGRAPHS BY
Jack Jeffrey
Brian E. Small, André F. Raine,
David Pereksta, Robby Kohley,
Jacob Drucker, Mike Danzenbaker,
Eric VanderWerf, and Others

Scott & Nix, Inc.
NEW YORK

A SCOTT & NIX EDITION

COPYRIGHT © 2020 BY HELEN AND ANDRÉ RAINE AND SCOTT & NIX, INC.

ALL RIGHTS RESERVED.

PUBLISHED BY SCOTT & NIX, INC.
150 W 28TH ST, STE 1900
NEW YORK, NY 10001
SCOTTANDNIX.COM

FIRST EDITION 2020

ISBN 978-1-935622-71-0

AMERICAN BIRDING ASSOCIATION®
AND ITS LOGO ARE REGISTERED TRADEMARKS OF
THE AMERICAN BIRDING ASSOCIATION, INC.
ALL RIGHTS RESERVED.

AMERICAN BIRDING ASSOCIATION, INC.
800-850-2473
ABA.ORG

SCOTT & NIX, INC. BOOKS
ARE DISTRIBUTED TO THE TRADE BY

INDEPENDENT PUBLISHERS GROUP (IPG)
814 NORTH FRANKLIN STREET
CHICAGO, IL 60610
800-888-4741
IPGBOOK.COM

THE PAPER OF THIS BOOK IS FSC CERTIFIED, WHICH
ASSURES IT WAS MADE FROM WELL MANAGED FORESTS
AND OTHER CONTROLLED SOURCES.

PRINTED IN CHINA

Contents

The American Birding Association inspires all people to enjoy and protect wild birds.

The ABA represents the North American birding community and supports birders through publications, conferences, workshops, events, partnerships, and networks.

The ABA's education programs promote birding skills, ornithological knowledge, and the development of and implementation of a conservation ethic.

The ABA encourages birders to apply their skills to help conserve birds and their habitats, and we represent the interests of birders in planning and legislative arenas.

We welcome all birders as members.

THE AMERICAN BIRDING ASSOCIATION
CODE OF ETHICS V. 2.1, NOVEMBER 2019

1. Respect and promote birds and their environment.

(a) Support the conservation of birds and their habitats. Engage in and promote bird-friendly practices whenever possible, such as keeping cats and other domestic animals indoors or controlled, acting to prevent window strikes, maintaining safe feeding stations, landscaping with native plants, drinking shade-grown coffee, and advocating for conservation policies. Be mindful of any negative environmental impacts of your activities, including contributing to climate change. Reduce or offset such impacts as much as you are able.

(b) Avoid stressing birds or exposing them to danger. Be particularly cautious around active nests and nesting colonies, roosts, display sites, and feeding sites. Limit the use of recordings and other audio methods of attracting birds, particularly in heavily birded areas, for species that are rare in the area, and for species that are threatened or endangered. Always exercise caution and restraint when photographing, recording, or otherwise approaching birds.

(c) Always minimize habitat disturbance. Consider the benefits of staying on trails, preserving snags, and similar practices. 2. Respect and promote the birding community and its individual members.

(a) Be an exemplary ethical role model by following this Code and leading by example. Always bird and report with honesty and integrity.

(b) Respect the interests, rights, and skill levels of fellow birders, as well as people participating in other outdoor activities. Freely share your knowledge and experience and be especially helpful to beginning birders.

(c) Share bird observations freely, provided such reporting would not violate other sections of this Code, as birders, ornithologists, and conservationists derive considerable benefit from publicly available bird sightings.

(d) Approach instances of perceived unethical birding behavior with sensitivity and respect; try to resolve the matter in a positive manner, keeping in mind that perspectives vary. Use the situation as an opportunity to teach by example and to introduce more people to this Code.

(e) In group birding situations, promote knowledge by everyone in the group of the practices in this Code and ensure that the group does not unduly interfere with others using the same area.

3. Respect and promote the law and the rights of others.

(a) Never enter private property without the landowner's permission. Respect the interests of and interact positively with people living in the area where you are birding.

(b) Familiarize yourself with and follow all laws, rules, and regulations governing activities at your birding location. In particular, be aware of regulations related to birds, such as disturbance of protected nesting areas or sensitive habitats, and the use of audio or food lures.

► Birding should be fun and help build a better future for birds, for birders, and for all people

► Birds and birding opportunities are shared resources that should be open and accessible to all

► Birders should always give back more than they take

Everyone who enjoys birds and birding must always respect wildlife, its environment, and the rights of others. The ABA Code of Ethics should be read, followed, and shared by all birders.

Please follow this code and distribute and teach it to others.

The American Birding Association's Code of Birding Ethics may be freely reproduced for distribution/dissemination. An electronic version may be found at www.aba.org/aba-code-of-birding-ethics/.

Foreword

Hawai'i is simply a paradise for birding offering a wealth of prime habitats for birds and outstanding opportunities for birders of all levels.

Like all the guides in this series, this book can help you do whatever you want with birding. Perhaps you enjoy birds a few days a year in your yard or local park and just want to know a little more about them and to know some of their names. Or maybe you want to dive deeper and really get familiar with the hundreds of amazing birds that call Hawai'i home for part or all of each year. Our aim is to meet you where you are and give you useful, reliable information and insight into birds and birding.

Authors André and Helen Raine are the perfect guides for those wanting to explore the birds of Hawai'i. You're in very good hands with them. The gorgeous photography by Jack Jeffrey and
others will not only aid your identifications—it will inspire you to get out and see more of these beautiful and fascinating creatures for yourself.

I invite you to visit the American Birding Association website (aba.org), where you'll find a wealth of free resources and ways to connect with the birding community that will also help you get the most from your birding in Hawai'i and beyond. Please consider becoming an ABA member yourself—one of the best parts of birding is joining a community of fun, passionate people.

Now get on out there! Enjoy this book. Enjoy Hawai'i. And most of all, enjoy birding!

Good birding,

Jeffrey A. Gordon, *President*
American Birding Association

Birds of Hawai‘i

Hawai‘i is a magical place for birdwatchers. The isolation of the archipelago, combined with its varied volcanic landscape, have created a spectacular and unique ecosystem. Hawai‘i is also home to at least 34 species of birds that are found nowhere else in the world, making it a must-see destination for birders.

Birdwatching in the Hawaiian Islands is unlike any birding experience on the U.S. mainland. The first thing you will notice is that the islands are heaving with introduced species from Asia, South America, Africa, and Europe. Many of the transplants are abundant, and most are easy to identify. Once you've gotten over the excitement of seeing so many exotics, you can focus on the real reason for birding here—the islands' endemics. Some can be tracked down easily but seeing the true rarities can be challenging. The payoff is spectacular scenery and the chance to add unique birds to your life list.

The Nēnē is Hawai‘i's official state bird and a conservation success story.

The non-natives tend to congregate in the lowlands, where you will also find the endemic waterbirds. Many hotels and golf courses on Kaua'i, for example, have the Hawaiian Common Gallinule ('Alae 'ula), Hawaiian Coot ('Alae ke'oke'o), and iconic Nēnē (Hawaiian Goose) pottering around water features and lawns. Migrant and wintering waders and waterfowl also frequent wetlands or coastal areas across the main Hawaiian Islands. The diversity of migratory species is not particularly rich, but you never know what may turn up.

As the elevation increases, the Hawaiian honeycreepers and other endemic forest birds become the focus. Most of the main islands have their own suite of endemics; to see them all, you will need to island-hop. Some of the birds are relatively easy to find; seeing others will require luck and a high degree of fitness; and some of the rarest species are restricted to virtually inaccessible protected areas.

Then there are the seabirds. Hawai'i is the most remote inhabited island chain in the world and has been a seabird haven for millennia. The Northwestern Hawaiian Islands have the largest colonies, but the main islands host significant colonies, too. Coastal watchpoints can provide great views of commuting seabirds. At dusk during the breeding season, the endemic Hawaiian Petrel ('Ua'u) and Newell's Shearwater ('A'o) fly overhead toward mountain breeding colonies, and offshore trips at the right time of year might turn up these two as well as an array of migrants.

Birds and Hawaiian Culture

Birds have always been an integral part of Hawaiian culture. For the early voyagers, who sailed across the Pacific in successive waves, the seabirds and the Pacific Golden-Plover (Kolea) were important guides that led the sailors toward islands that were too small to see. With the birds' help, Hawai'i was discovered. Seabirds have also been key for fishermen who follow feeding flocks to predatory fish like ahi (tuna) and ono (wahoo).

After the Polynesians settled in Hawai'i, items made from the feathers of both seabirds and landbirds became symbols of high rank and great accomplishment as Hawaiian culture developed. Feather images were consulted as oracles for the gods. White feather lei from the Laysan Albatross (Mōlī) were hung on the Makahiki celebration banner as kinolau (embodiments) of Lono, the god of peace and agriculture. To this day, one of the highest gifts a person can receive is a feather lei, an 'ahu'ula (cape), a mahiole (helmet), or a kahili (standard) made from the feathers of a Hawaiian bird.

Birds and their imagery are also invoked in numerous Hawaiian songs and chants, often when someone is speaking poetically about a loved one. A classic example is: *'Auhea Wale 'Oe E Ka 'Ō'ō/Manu Leo Nahe O Ka Uka* (Where are you 'Ō'ō bird?/ Sweet-voiced bird of the forest). This is a chant that honors Queen Emma Kaleleonālani and sadly relates to the now extinct 'Ō'ō.

Lastly, several bird species are considered to be 'aumakua, or family guardian spirits. 'Aumakua can take the form of a bird such as the Hawaiian Short-eared Owl (Pueo), the I'iwi, or an 'Elepaio and help guide family members through visions and dreams, keeping manu (birds) deeply intertwined in Hawaiian life and culture.

—Kumu Sabra Kauka, Hawaiian Cultural Practitioner

Kumu Sabra Kauka releases a rescued Newell's Shearwater ('A'o) at a ceremony on Kaua'i.

Bird Conservation in Hawai‘i

Millions of years ago, the first finches landed on Hawaiian soil.
Over time, they evolved into different species, following the
same process that created 14 species of Darwin's finches in the
Galapagos Islands. In Hawai‘i, however, Mother Nature went
into overdrive: at least 56 different honeycreeper species
evolved from one or two common ancestors.

The new honeycreepers developed a range of features perfectly
suited to the plants they came to exploit. For example, the I‘iwi
evolved a curved bill to access the nectar of equally curved
lobelia flowers. New species of thrush, rail, crow, waterbird,
and seabird also evolved. They lived in the middle of the Pacific
in a world with no terrestrial predators, a different suite of
birds on each isolated island. Some lost the ability to fly. Others
lost their sense of danger.

The arrival of humans (Polynesians and then Europeans) shook
up this unusual ecosystem. Birds were used for food and
decoration, and mammalian predators were introduced. Rats,
cats, and pigs began to prey on the largely defenseless birds,
resulting in the rapid extinction of more than 70 species,
including various flightless rails, moa-nalo (large goose-like

Endemic honeycreepers, like
this critically endangered
‘Akikiki on Kaua‘i, are being
decimated by introduced
avian malaria.

ducks), stilt-owls, black and yellow mamos, and ʻŌ ʻōs.
High elevation habitats became the last refuge for many
endemic species.

Today the single biggest threat to most of Hawaiʻi's forest birds
is avian malaria. No blood-sucking insects lived in the islands
before Europeans brought mosquito larvae in their water
barrels. Mosquitos spread the avian malaria parasite from
introduced birds to native forest birds, which have little
natural immunity. The introduction of huge numbers of exotic
bird species by the Hui Manu, or "introductions society"
(formed in 1930), compounded the problem.

Introduced predators continue to threaten all Hawaiian birds,
and relatively new additions such as the small Indian mongoose
heighten the danger. In the lowlands, colonies of abandoned
cats prey on ground-nesting seabirds and waterbirds. Feral
dogs also decimate seabird colonies, killing Laysan Albatross
Mōlī) and Wedge-tailed Shearwaters (ʻUaʻu kani) by the dozen.

Endemic seabirds, birds that evolved in a dark world, also
suffer because of nighttime lighting. When chicks make their
first flight from the mountains to the ocean, they become
distracted by artificial lights, which the birds circle until they

Seabirds evolved on the
Hawaiian Islands without
mammalian predators, making
species like the Newell's
Shearwater vulnerable to cats,
rats, and pigs.

hit the ground. Unable to get airborne again, they usually die unless they are rescued. Endangered seabirds hit powerlines too, particularly Kaua'i, resulting in over one thousand deaths a year on that island alone.

Other threats include the spread of noxious weeds (especially strawberry guava and Himalayan ginger) and Rapid 'Ōhi'a Death, which has already killed hundreds of thousands of trees across the state. This is alarming as the 'Ōhi'a is the dominant tree in native forests. You can help by scrubbing your boots with rubbing alcohol when moving between forest areas (removing invasive seeds at the same time).

Resetting the Balance

Bird extinctions in Hawai'i are unfortunately not a thing of the past. The last Po'ouli was seen in 2004, and the 'Akikiki, Kiwikiu (Maui Parrotbill), and several other species teeter on the edge. Their catastrophic declines have galvanized Hawai'i's conservationists, who are attempting to restore native and endemic bird species across the islands.

Their efforts have focused on restoring forests and releasing rare captive-bred forest birds into restored landscapes. In the

After extensive restoration work on Laysan Island, Millerbirds were reintroduced in 2011–2012 and the population has started to expand.

mountains, intensive control programs are removing predators using innovative technologies such as automatically resetting rat traps. At the same time, seabirds are being translocated from the mountains to predator-proof enclosures on the coast. To protect seabirds from sea-level rise, species are also being translocated from the Northwestern Hawaiian Islands to the main islands. And landscape-level solutions for avian malaria are being investigated, including the use of a bacterium that is harmless to humans and birds but suppresses mosquito populations by creating sterile males.

Some remarkable success stories have already been told. The Nēnē is the poster bird for our ability to turn around populations on the brink of extinction. Only about 40 Hawaiian Geese remained in the 1950s due to predation, hunting, and habitat loss, but today, thanks to conservation efforts, there are now around 2,800. In addition, the ʻAlalā (Hawaiian Crow) has been reintroduced to the wild after a decade of captive breeding. In 2019, it was recorded nesting in the wild for the first time in over 20 years. These successes show that with the right amount of perseverance, funding, political will, and innovation, it is possible to change the tide, ensuring that we can continue to appreciate these amazing species into the future.

Once extinct in the wild, the ʻAlalā (Hawaiian Crow) is making a comeback and in 2016, captive bred birds were released back into the wild.

Birds in this Guide

The current bird list for the Hawaiian Islands totals 338 species, but many are rare vagrants that have been recorded only a handful of times. The purpose of this guidebook is not to cover every species ever recorded in Hawai'i. Rather, we describe birds you are likely to see when you visit, as well as the Hawaiian specialties. (For a full checklist see page 160.)

We provide full accounts for 139 birds, including all 34 remaining endemic species and subspecies and all native breeding species. Our focus is the main Hawaiian Islands, but we also include endemics and natives found only in the northwestern islands. All common migrants and winter visitors and the more frequently recorded vagrants are considered. Lastly, we provide accounts for almost all introduced species. Many are abundant throughout the archipelago, and for better or worse, you will certainly become familiar with them.

How to Use the Species Accounts

All of the accounts start with each bird's common, Hawaiian, and scientific names. Where the Hawaiian name is in more common use, it appears first. A good example is the Nēnē, see pages 4–5. The scientific name consists of two words, the genus and species, and follows the format accepted by the American Ornithological Society. Entries appear in the same order as species on the American Birding Association checklist. For species where there is an endemic subspecies in Hawai'i, we include the subspecies name.

Next we present the status of species in Hawai'i. The authoritative source is *The Birds of the Hawaiian Islands: Occurrence, History, Distribution, and Status* by Robert L. Pyle and Peter Pyle, published in 2017 by the Bishop Museum in Honolulu. It lists the following status designations:

ENDEMIC Found in the Hawaiian Islands and nowhere else (e.g., Newell's Shearwater, see page 81)

NATIVE Breeds in the Hawaiian Islands after having arrived without human intervention (e.g., Laysan Albatross, see page 68)

INTRODUCED Breeds in the Hawaiian Islands after having been brought by humans (e.g., Java Sparrow, see page 125)

MIGRANT Found in the Hawaiian Islands only during migration (e.g., Sooty Shearwater, see page 77)

WINTER VISITOR Migrates to the Hawaiian Islands and then overwinters (e.g., Pacific Golden-Plover, see page 36)

VAGRANT An irregular, not annual, visitor to the Hawaiian Islands (e.g., Snow Goose, see page 2)

For species that are of conservation concern, we also note their global conservation status, as found on the Red List of Threatened Species published by the International Union for the Conservation of Nature (iucnredlist.org). Where the Red List does not provide an assessment, we use U.S. Fish and Wildlife Service designations (e.g., for endemic subspecies like the Hawaiian Common Gallinule).

Unless indicated otherwise, the main Hawaiian Islands include Kaua'i, O'ahu, Maui, Lāna'i, Moloka'i, and Hawai'i Island. Kaho'olawe and Ni'ihau are generally excluded due to a dearth of information about bird life there. The islets are referred to by their first name only, e.g. Ka'ula rather than Ka'ula Rock.

To help with identification in the field, average length (L) and wingspan (WS) measurements are given where available to provide an overall impression of a bird's size.

We describe the bird's song or call if it is useful for identification but do not do so for many migrants or winter visitors that are predominantly silent in Hawai'i. Each account has a photo or several showing the best identification features. Photos taken in Hawai'i are prioritized, although for some species photos were taken elsewhere.

Key Features of a Bird

If you are just starting out as a birdwatcher, you may find yourself staring aghast at some of the terminology used to describe a bird. While everyone is familiar with what a wing or a tail is, conversations among birders can include more technical terms. In our species accounts, we try to steer clear of the minutiae of bird identification. However, a basic understanding of the parts of a bird is important if, for example, you want to tell an 'Apapane (see page 136) from an I'iwi (see page 138). Photographs in the next pages show examples of four basic bird groups: waterfowl, seabirds, raptors, and passerines (perching birds). Familiarize yourself with the birds' bits and pieces, and you will soon find yourself holding forth on prominent superciliums (eyebrow stripes) or metallic green speculums (patches of brightly colored feathers on the upper wing).

Koloa Maoli (Hawaiian Duck)

Pueo
(Short-eared Owl)

primaries

secondaries

leading edge

breast

'Io (Hawaiian Hawk)

back

nape

crown

forehead

secondaries

primaries

tail

talons

throat

breast

primaries

secondaries

back

rump

tail

crown

forehead

bill

trailing edge

leading edge

throat

Bonin Petrel

'I'iwi

nape
crown
back
bill
secondaries
primaries
throat
tail
vent
breast

nape
eye line
supercilium
lore
throat

Kiwikiu (Maui Parrotbill)

Birdwatching in the Hawaiian Islands

To help you get the most out of your birding visit, we have provided a selection of some of the best birding locations on each of the main Hawaiian islands. These sites will give you the best chance of finding the key endemics. This is not a complete list of birding sites but you should try to at least visit these during your trip. Enjoy tracking down our special bird species—finding them is half the fun.

If you can manage to visit only two islands, Kaua'i and Hawai'i Island are probably the best. Kaua'i is free of small Indian mongoose and still relatively rural and compact in size, so you can tick off lots of birds swiftly. Hawai'i Island has not only a wide range of endemics but also amazing coral reefs and smoldering active volcanoes.

Kaua'i

Kōke'e State Park (especially the Pihea Trail and Alaka'i Swamp Trail)—A misty rainforest area, Kōke'e is the place on Kaua'i for endemic forest birds. All of the island's forest birds live here, including the endangered rarities Puaiohi, 'Akikiki, and 'Akeke'e. Sightings of those three are very challenging, but seeing the other natives is usually straightforward. You can access the eerie beauty of the Alaka'i Swamp on a boardwalk. Flowering 'ōhi'a trees on the perimeter often harbor endemics. Between April and September, hang out at the Pu'u O Kila lookout at nightfall; listen for Newell's Shearwaters and Hawaiian Petrels calling en route to montane breeding colonies.

Kīlauea Point National Wildlife Refuge—This refuge holds large populations of breeding seabirds, including the Laysan Albatross (Mōlī), Red-footed Booby ('Ā), and Wedge-tailed Shearwater ('Ua'u kani), while Great Frigatebirds ('Iwa) soar overhead. You should get sightings of Nēnē, and it is a great watchpoint for seabirds.

Hanalei National Wildlife Refuge—This large area of taro fields and wetlands holds all the native waterbirds and migratory waterfowl and waders. At the Hanalei Bridge, take Ohiki Road and park near the Okolehao trailhead. Access to the wetlands is restricted to that entry road, but you can see birds from there.

Kawaiʻele Waterbird Sanctuary—Located on the west side of Kauaʻi, this sanctuary has a range of waterfowl and waders, especially during migration and winter.

Oʻahu

Kaʻena Point State Park—Protected on three sides by a predator-proof fence, this is an important area for the Laysan Albatross and Wedge-tailed Shearwater.

James Campbell National Wildlife Refuge—Native and migratory waterbirds, including the Bristle-thighed Curlew (Kioea), visit this refuge. The Kahuku Aqua Ponds are especially good. This is also the site of a translocation project for the Bonin's Petrel, Tristram's Storm-Petrel, and two species of albatross from the Northwestern Hawaiian Islands. Admittance is by special appointment only.

The mist enshrouded Alakaʻi Swamp on Kauaʻi is home to all of the island's endangered forest birds, including the Critically Endangered Puaiohi

Makapu'u Point—An accessible point to look for seabirds offshore and along the coastline.

'Aiea Loop Trail—This easy trail might have views of the Mariana Swiftlet and O'ahu 'Elepaio, as well as introduced passerines.

Maui

Keālia Pond National Wildlife Refuge—700 acres of protected wetlands host native waterbirds and migrants. The site includes coastal habitat and an easy-access boardwalk.

Kanaha Pond State Wildlife Sanctuary—Next to Kahului Airport, this is an accessible area for native or migrant waterbirds and waterfowl.

Haleakalā National Park—Hawaiian Petrels breed on this iconic summit. You may hear them calling after dark or before dawn. The 'Ākohekohe, Kiwikiu, and Hawai'i 'Amakihi are present in the forests on Haleakalā's slopes along with other honey-creepers; check out Hosmer's Grove and Waikamoi Preserve (the latter only accessible via guided hikes with The Nature Conservancy).

With its multi-colored plumage and spectacular crest, the 'Ākohekohe is a sought-after species in Haleakalā National Park on Maui.

Molokini—A volcanic islet three miles off the southeastern coast of Maui, Molokini holds breeding colonies of Wedge-tailed Shearwater and Bulwer's Petrel ('Ou) and is accessible by boat tour. The snorkeling is great, too.

Lāna'i

Munroe Trail—Rising through misty native forest on the flanks of the Lāna'ihale mountain, the Munroe Trail is home to Lāna'i's endemic snails and the Hawaiian Petrel. You might see petrels flying up to their colonies after dusk from April to October.

Hulopoe—Wedge-tailed Shearwaters nest in a sprawling colony on the headland next to Hulopoe Beach Park. Stick to designated trails to avoid collapsing their burrows. Look from the cliffs toward Pu'u Pehe (Sweetheart Rock) for seabirds.

Lāna'i Sewage Treatment Plant—Not exactly a tourist hotspot, this is nonetheless a great place to see Hawaiian Stilts and Hawaiian Coots, as well as migratory waders and waterfowl.

Hawaiian Petrels nest in deep burrows in the uluhe covered slopes on either side of the Munroe Trail on Lāna'i

Moloka'i

Kamakou Preserve—Accessible only via a four-wheeled-drive vehicle or on guided walks with The Nature Conservancy, this protected area has some of Moloka'i's last native forests. You can spot the Hawai'i 'Amakihi and 'Apapane, and the last recorded sightings of the Moloka'i Creeper and Oloma'o were here. Both are now presumed extinct.

Kakahai'a National Wildlife Refuge—Created to protect an area of coastal wetlands, Kakahai'a is a good place to see the Hawaiian Coot and Hawaiian Stilt, as well as migratory waterfowl.

Mo'omomi Preserve—Another of The Nature Conservancy's protected areas, Mo'omomi covers an important coastal dune ecosystem. There is a breeding colony of Wedge-tailed Shearwaters, and the Hawaiian Short-eared Owl (Pueo) might be seen over the grasslands. The Nature Conservancy offers guided walks.

Hawai'i Island

Hawai'i Volcanoes National Park—Smoking craters, lava flows, and mist-shrouded native forest make this a great place for scenery and birds. Look for the 'Ōma'o, I'iwi, and 'Apapane. Check the

Mo'omomi Preserve on Moloka'i has a large breeding colony of Wedge-tailed Shearwaters as well as other species.

National Park website before visiting, as areas are sometimes closed due to volcanic activity.

Hakalau Forest National Wildlife Refuge—A large protected area on the windward slopes of Maunakea, Hakalau Forest has a wide range of habitats. Most of the island's endemic forest birds can be spotted here, including the ʻAkiapōlāʻau, ʻŌmaʻo, Hawaiʻi ʻAkepa, and Hawaiʻi Creeper. ʻIo can be seen circling overhead. The refuge is only accessible via guided hikes. Contact the U.S. Fish & Wildlife Service for information about visiting.

Puʻu ʻŌʻō Trail—Accessed via the Saddle Road (between mile markers 22 and 23), this trail winds across lava fields and kīpuka (small pockets of forest surrounded by lava). In those forest oases, you can spot endemic birds, including (if you are lucky) the ʻAkiapōlāʻau, ʻAkepa, and Hawaiʻi Creeper. The lava fields may afford views of the Hawaiian Short-eared Owl (Pueo).

Palila Discovery Trail—This one-mile loop will lead you through dry forests dominated by māmane and naio on the slopes of Maunakea. The trees are the favored food of the Palila, so look for the main islands' last finch-billed honeycreeper here.

The extraordinary ʻAkiapōlāʻau is found only on Hawaiʻi Island. Look for it and other endemics on the Puʻu ʻŌʻō Trail.

American Birding Association

Field Guide to
Birds of Hawai'i

Snow Goose

Anser caerulescens

L 30"   **WS** 54"

VAGRANT

The Snow Goose breeds in the tundra of Siberia and the North American Arctic and flies south across Canada, the United States, and Mexico in winter. A vagrant in Hawai'i, it can show up on any of the islands in a wide range of habitats, including wetlands, golf courses, and coastal areas. Sightings appear to be increasing, perhaps because breeding populations are growing. Snow Geese are found in two color morphs: white and blue (or dark). To date, all Snow Geese recorded in Hawai'i have been white morphs. They utter high, barking calls: *howk howk howk*.

Large white goose with black primaries. Thick pink bill and pink legs. Juvenile grayish, with dark legs and bill.

Cackling Goose
Branta hutchinsii

L 26"   **WS** 43"

WINTER VISITOR

Much smaller than the closely related Canada Goose, the Cackling Goose breeds in the tundra of northern Canada and Alaska. A few individuals can be spotted in Hawai'i almost every year while migrating to their wintering grounds, particularly in fall. Some may overwinter. One goose, banded in 2005, has wintered annually at Kīlauea Point National Wildlife Refuge on Kaua'i for 18 years to date. Calls consist of high-pitched or squeaky honks and cackles (hence the name).

Rounded black head and short neck, white chin strap. Grayish brown body, white under tail.

Nēnē (Hawaiian Goose)
Branta sandvicensis

L 22-26"   **WS** 43-47"

ENDEMIC, VULNERABLE

This medium-sized goose is the state bird of Hawai'i and one of its greatest conservation success stories. Only about 40 birds remained by the 1950s, but captive breeding on Hawai'i Island, in Connecticut, and in England kickstarted a recovery. Now there are approximately 2,800 individuals statewide. Kaua'i is a stronghold; its population has been used as a source for birds translocated to other islands. At least nine native goose species once lived on the Hawaiian Islands. Only the Nēnē survived; the rest were flightless and were quickly wiped out after the arrival of humans. Nēnē evolved from Canada Geese but are smaller, with less webbing between their toes and a buff neck. Vocalizations are high querulous honks and a low call that sounds like their name: *ne ne*. May also hiss if threatened.

This goose utilizes a wide range of natural habitats as well as golf courses and suburban lawns.

Medium-sized brown goose. Black face and crown, buff neck with black streaks. Heavily barred brown flanks and back. Sexes alike.

Fiercely protective parents, they have up to five goslings. They are vulnerable to predators and vehicle collisions.

Blue-winged Teal
Spatula discors

L 15" | **WS** 23"

WINTER VISITOR, FORMER BREEDER

These small dabbling ducks breed across North America, with strongholds in the prairies of the central United States and Canada, and migrate to South America for the winter. They can turn up on any of the main Hawaiian Islands in appropriate habitat, although they are only an occasional winter visitor. A pair bred for two consecutive years on Hawai'i Island (1982–83), producing up to 11 chicks, and breeding was suspected on Kaua'i in 2016. Teal prefer shallow wetlands or flooded fields, where they seek out seeds, aquatic plants, and invertebrates from the surface or just below, rarely upending.

Male with bluish gray head, white crescent in front of gray bill, brown body. Pale blue forewing, green speculum. Female (below) pale brown.

Northern Shoveler (Koloa Moha)

Spatula clypeata

L 18" | **WS** 30"

WINTER VISITOR

Another relatively common wintering species, these dabbling ducks can turn up on any of the main islands. They usually arrive in October and depart for their breeding grounds by April or May. That they are one of only two migratory duck species with a Hawaiian name indicates their strong connection with the archipelago. Their large, flat bill is perfect for scooping up and filtering aquatic invertebrates like water fleas and crustaceans, but shovelers also eat snails and seeds. They can be found in any large water body during winter but prefer shallow ponds and marshes.

Long shovel-like bill. Male with metallic green head, white chest, chestnut sides. Pale blue forewing, green speculum.

Pale brown with large orange, shovel-like bill. Green speculum, gray forewing, white underwing. Orange legs.

Eurasian Wigeon

Mareca penelope

L 20" | **WS** 32"

WINTER VISITOR

A handful of Eurasian Wigeon usually appear in the main
islands on migration every year, sometimes in the company
of American Wigeon, and some will stay the whole winter
season. They appear less frequently on the Northwestern
Hawaiian Islands, but multiple sightings of the species have
been recorded. These medium-sized dabbling ducks breed in
northern Europe and Asia. Females can be difficult to distin-
guish from the closely related American Wigeon, but males are
distinctive, with a chestnut-colored head and pale gray body.
Eurasians prefer open wetlands with some taller vegetation
and will dabble for aquatic plants or graze.

Male with chestnut head, buff
forehead, pale gray body and
wings. White patch on forewing,
dark green speculum.

Female rufous-brown.

American Wigeon

Mareca americana

L 20″ | **WS** 33″

WINTER VISITOR

The American Wigeon breeds in northern North America, preferring tundra and boreal forest habitats. One of the most common migratory ducks, it winters annually in small numbers in Hawai'i and can turn up in the right habitat on any island. These dabbling ducks are mainly vegetarian and have a powerful biting bill, designed to cut through aquatic plants efficiently. In Hawai'i, they are fond of taro patches and will also graze, mainly at night, on fields and lawns. They are nicknamed "baldpate" after the male's distinctive crown.

Male with pale gray-brown head, white forehead, glossy green patch behind eye. White patch on wing, green speculum.

Female with gray-brown head.

Laysan Duck
Anas laysanensis

L 16"

ENDEMIC, CRITICALLY ENDANGERED

The fossilized bones of this dabbling duck have been found throughout the main islands, but its range was reduced to Laysan in the Northwestern Hawaiian Islands after the Polynesians arrived. It almost went extinct there due to a combination of hunting and habitat loss caused by introduced European rabbits. Rabbits were removed in 1923, and Laysan Ducks were translocated to Midway in the mid-2000s and Kure in 2015. The current population fluctuates around 750 birds. Laysan Ducks eat aquatic vegetation and insects, which they catch by speeding through clouds of brine flies with an open, snapping bill. Their call is a soft, buzzing *quack*.

Dark brown. Large irregular white patch around eye and bill base. Bill greenish on male, dull orange on female. Purple or blue-green speculum.

Mallard (Kaka)

Anas platyrhynchos

L 22" | **WS** 34"

WINTER VISITOR, INTRODUCED

Mallards in Hawai'i consist of two groups: migratory birds that occasionally overwinter and, far more common, feral birds that have naturalized throughout the islands. The feral Mallards hybridize with the endemic and endangered Koloa Maoli (Hawaiian Duck), causing serious conservation problems. Consequently, Koloa populations on O'ahu and Maui are now largely composed of hybrids. Mallards use a "nail" on their bill to collect prey and can be found throughout wetland habitats. Their call is the familiar *quack quack*; females are louder, males more rasping.

Male with dark green head, white collar, yellow bill, chestnut chest, gray body. Curly black tail feathers.

Female brown. White-bordered blue speculum.

Koloa Maoli (Hawaiian Duck)

Anas wyvilliana

L 20"

ENDEMIC, ENDANGERED

This Hawaiian endemic looks like a small female Mallard. Its range has contracted severely due to loss of wetland habitat, predation, and sport hunting (now illegal). The population reached a low of about 500 individuals in the 1940s, but wetland conservation has resulted in a minimum of 1,000 birds in the wild today. Hybridization (interbreeding of two different species) with Mallards is one of the species' biggest challenges. Around 80 percent of the population is on Kaua'i, where rates of hybridization remain low. They are also found on Hawai'i Island, Maui, and O'ahu (although they are mainly hybrids on the latter two islands). The birds use taro fields, ponds, marshes, and streams, including mountain streams and Kaua'i's high-altitude Alaka'i Swamp. They have a varied diet, eating wetland vegetation, snails, worms, and flying insects, and utter a soft, buzzy *quack*.

Small, slender duck with brown plumage. White-bordered emerald-green to blue speculum. Male has darker head and neck.

Both sexes similar to small female Mallard but with dark bill, and dark undertail feathers.

One of the biggest conservation challenges facing this species is hybridization with Mallards. The best place to find purebred Koloa Maoli (shown here) is the island of Kaua'i.

Northern Pintail (Koloa Māpu)

Anas acuta

L 21" | **WS** 34"

WINTER VISITOR

This attractive, slender dabbling duck is a common winter visitor and can appear in appropriate habitat on any of the main Hawaiian Islands. Pintails are present from August until late March or April, when they leave for breeding grounds in Canada, Alaska, or Siberia. They prefer freshwater but can also be found in brackish ponds. Their diet consists of aquatic grasses and invertebrates. Pintail numbers in Hawai'i have been declining over the past few decades, a trend also seen across North America, due to the loss of wetland habitat and hunting.

Male with chestnut head, white neck, pale gray body. Long black tail streamers.

Female pale brown with long neck. White-edged, greenish bronze speculum.

Green-winged Teal

Anas crecca

L 14" **WS** 23"

WINTER VISITOR

These diminutive, dabbling ducks are winter visitors that arrive in small numbers from mid-September to April and can appear on any of the main islands in appropriate habitat. They congregate with other waterfowl in freshwater areas such as lakes, ponds, shrimp farms, and water features on golf courses. They tip up to feed in shallow water or snatch at food while standing in flooded fields. Two of the Green-winged Teal's three subspecies, the Eurasian and the American, have been recorded on the islands. The American is seen more commonly.

Male with chestnut head, green patch behind eye, gray body.

Female pale brown with yellowish streak below tail. Green speculum.

Ring-necked Duck

Aythya collaris

L 17"   **WS** 25"

WINTER VISITOR

Regular winter visitors, these medium-sized diving ducks breed in a range of habitats from subarctic to prairie regions of North America and winter in Central and South America. They can arrive in the main Hawaiian Islands at any time from late September onward and appear throughout winter in freshwater habitats. There is evidence that individual birds return to the same place in subsequent years. Pay special attention to the key identification features, as Ring-necked Ducks can be confused with Tufted Ducks and Greater and Lesser Scaup.

Male with black head, back, and breast, pale gray sides. Black-tipped bill with white band.

Female brown with white eye ring.

Lesser Scaup

Aythya affinis

L 16-17" | **WS** 25-26"

WINTER VISITOR

Regular winter visitors to Hawai'i, these attractive diving ducks arrive around October and return to breed in the boreal forests in Alaska and Canada in February. They can turn up on any of the main islands, where they can be seen among flocks of other ducks in freshwater or brackish locations like ponds and inlets. They eat aquatic plants, mollusks, and aquatic invertebrates, all of which they take while diving under water. Easily confused with the less common Greater Scaup, they have a narrower, more purplish head with a peak and a longer-looking neck.

Male with dark purple head, pale gray back, and white sides. Narrow black bill tip. White wing stripe extends halfway on wing.

Female dark brown with white at base of bill. Thick white wing stripe.

California Quail

Callipepla californica

L 10" | **WS** 13.5"

INTRODUCED

Originally from North America, the California Quail was brought to Hawai'i in 1818 as a gift to King Kamehameha from Vasiliy Golovnin, a Russian navigator. Populations became established throughout the main islands (apart from Lāna'i), but their sizes are uncertain, and they have since been extirpated on O'ahu. The largest populations are found on Hawai'i Island and Moloka'i. This is a cryptic, skulking species; flocks will explode out of the bush in different directions when disturbed. The scientific name means "beautifully dressed." The birds utter a high-pitched, surprised *ahr* and a loud, three-syllable call: *Chi-ca-go*.

Small game bird with prominent head plume. Male slate gray with white-bordered black face, scaled neck.

Female with pale gray head.

Chukar

Alectoris chukar

L 13.5-15" | **WS** 21"

INTRODUCED

The natural range of this attractive game bird spans eastern Europe, Asia, and the Middle East. It was introduced across all of the main Hawaiian Islands between 1942 and 1954 with varying levels of success. Chukar are now found mainly in upland areas up to 11,000 feet on Hawai'i Island, Maui, and Lāna'i. A skulking bird, the Chukar tends to lay low and flush when approached, although birds in some areas (such as Haleakalā National Park) can be remarkably confiding. Their wide array of calls includes a grating, repetitive clucking: *chu-chu-chu-chu-chukar-chukar* (reminiscent of chickens).

Chunky pale gray game bird. Black band through eye extending to necklace. Red bill and feet. Heavy black barring on sides.

Gray Francolin

Francolinus pondicerianus

L 13" | **WS** 53–63"

INTRODUCED

Originally from India and the Middle East, Gray Francolins were introduced to Hawai'i in 1958 for game-bird hunting. Though not as common as the larger Erckel's Francolin, they can be found on all of the main islands except Ni'ihau and Kaho'olawe. They prefer drier shrubland and savannah habitat in leeward and coastal areas but also do well in plantations and golf courses; you might see them on hotel lawns too, especially in the early morning or late evening. Listen for courting birds singing duets. Typical calls start out with high *checks*, followed by frantic, high-pitched, repetitive three-tone *ka tee tar* calls.

Small, slender, gray-brown game bird. Orange forehead, cheeks, and throat. Gray bill, pinkish brown legs. Sexes alike.

Black Francolin

Francolinus francolinus

L 13-14" **WS** 20-21.5"

INTRODUCED

This diminutive game bird has a wide-ranging natural distribution from Cyprus to Myanmar but was introduced to the Aloha State as a game bird in the late 1950s. It is present on all of the main islands, either as a result of deliberate introductions or, in the case of Lāna'i, after flying from neighboring islands. It likes dry habitats with plenty of cover and tends to skulk when disturbed, rather than flying. A secretive species, the Black Francolin can sometimes be seen near roadsides, particularly early or late in the day. It has a raspy, five-syllable call, the last three tones rushed together: *beep beep be-di-beep*.

Male (shown) with black head and chest, white cheek, reddish brown neck, white-spotted flanks. Female pale brown with reddish brown nape.

Erckel's Francolin

Francolinus erckelii

L 16"

INTRODUCED

Since their introduction as a game bird from northeastern Africa in 1957, Erckel's Francolins have proliferated on most of the islands (apart from Maui and Moloka'i, where their status is uncertain) and are the most conspicuous of our francolin species. Though fond of dry, open areas, they are also distributed in wet montane forests, lowlands, even golf courses. The birds typically run when disturbed, rather than flying. Their diet includes berries, seeds, and insects. They have a loud and strident call, consisting of laughing, nasal *ha ha ha ha* that accelerates toward the end.

Largest francolin in Hawai'i. Pale gray, heavily streaked reddish brown. Reddish brown cap, dark gray face, white throat. Sexes alike.

Red Junglefowl (Mua/Moa)

Gallus gallus

L 17"   **WS** 20"

INTRODUCED

The Red Junglefowl is the ancestor of the domestic chicken and is native to Southeast Asia. It was introduced to the main Hawaiian Islands around AD 500–700 by the Polynesians, for whom it was an important source of food. Recent studies have shown that pure junglefowl are now relatively rare and extirpated from most of the islands, having interbred with domestic chickens, but Kaua'i remains a stronghold, with populations in Kōke'e State Park and the Alaka'i Swamp. Elsewhere, the hybrid descendants of the Red Junglefowl are more plentiful, annoying residents with their loud, nocturnal crowing and wandering in large numbers through residential areas.

Large impressive-looking chicken. Male (shown) archetypal rooster: golden-brown neck and back, metallic green chest and tail. White rump. Red comb.

Kalij Pheasant
Lophura leucomelanos

L 20-28" | **WS** 20"

INTRODUCED

Introduced to Hawai'i Island in 1962, these game bird have also been sighted on O'ahu and Maui, although their status there is uncertain. In their native central Asia, they live in pairs or small harems, but their behavior on Hawai'i is changing. Here, they are sometimes found in large, social groups of one female, several males, and a host of young birds; this is an unusual example of cooperative breeding in pheasants. Like other game birds, they spread the seeds of invasive plants such as banana poka. They make rapid, startled, soft clucks, whistles, and grunts.

Male (shown) black with silver chest and sides. Red face, long black crest, thick black tail. Female brown with red face, brown tail.

Ring-necked Pheasant

Phasianus colchicus

L 24-35" | **WS** 28-31"

INTRODUCED

Perhaps the ultimate game bird, this species was first introduced to Oʻahu in the 1860s at the request of King Kamehameha V. It is now distributed across all of the main Hawaiian Islands and is commonly hunted. Its feathers often adorn the hats of paniolo (cowboys). Ring-necked Pheasants are common in open areas such as fields, especially those bordered by bushes, up to 11,000 feet. The males establish territories in spring and will defend them violently, jumping at rivals with claws and spurs. Females lay up to 15 eggs in a nest depression. They make a loud, harsh, two-syllable *uur-urk* that can carry long distances.

Male typically golden brown with long tail, purple neck, and red face. White neck band. Female (left) pale brown, heavily flecked.

Wild Turkey

Meleagris gallopavo

L 42"   **WS** 53"

INTRODUCED

You might be surprised to find a turkey in the tropical vegetation of Hawai'i, but this is not a Thanksgiving hallucination. Twenty birds were brought from China in 1788, making the Wild Turkey one of the first species introduced to the main Hawaiian Islands after European contact. The biggest population is now found on Hawai'i Island, where this quintessential American bird can be seen everywhere, from the manicured grounds of hotels to the slopes of Maunakea. Populations are also on Lāna'i, Moloka'i, Ni'ihau, and Maui, although they have disappeared from O'ahu and Kaua'i. The bird makes a classic *gobble gobble* sound and also short *chucks*.

Large, chunky game bird. Male larger than female with pale red and blue head and heavy red wattles. Female slenderer, without heavy wattles.

Pied-billed Grebe

Podilymbus podiceps

L 13.5"   **WS** 21"

VAGRANT, FORMER BREEDER

This species established a small breeding population on Hawai'i Island for a short time between 1985 and 1993. The breeding birds eventually disappeared, possibly due in part to an outbreak of botulism. The species is now recorded in the main Hawaiian Islands as a vagrant, showing up in winter on quiet ponds and marshes and leaving again in spring. Pied-billed Grebes are expert divers that use lobed feet to power down and catch fish or crustaceans. Their name comes from the black band present around the bill in the breeding season. They utter a lengthy series of bouncing *how how how* sounds.

Small brown grebe with relatively large head. Black stripe on gray bill disappears in winter. White under tail.

Chestnut-bellied Sandgrouse

Pterocles exustus

L 12" | **WS** 19-20"

INTRODUCED

Normally found from sub-Saharan Africa to India but introduced to Hawai'i Island, Kaua'i, and Moloka'i in the 1960s, Chestnut-bellied Sandgrouse are now found only on Hawai'i Island, mainly in the northwest, in dry grassland areas, especially near watering holes. They feed on the seeds of grasses and weeds. Surprisingly powerful fliers, the birds can make headway even in the strong Waimea winds; they also get up onto the Saddle Road, as high as 5,000 feet. Sandgrouse carry water to chicks in their breast feathers, an amazing adaptation for arid climates. Calls are bubbling and repetitive, a worried *brip, blip* or *blip-di-brip.*

Male tan with orange cast to head and wings. Chestnut belly and thighs, dark breast band. Female tan, heavily streaked.

Spotted Dove

Streptopelia chinensis

L 12" | **WS** 21"

INTRODUCED

Originally from Southeast Asia, this large dove was introduced to Hawai'i in the 1860s for sport shooting and is now found throughout the main islands. Spotted Doves occupy a wide range of habitats and are very common in urban areas and gardens, where they tend to remain in pairs as they search for seeds and fruit. They breed year-round; males put on alluring aerial displays with noisy wing claps. When percehd, they coo, bow, and flare their tails to impress females. Their call is a repetitive, hoarse *Hroo-Hroo-Hrooo*.

Large, chunky dove. Black nape, heavily spotted white. Pale gray head, pink-tinged breast. Juvenile lack collar and are duller.

Zebra Dove (Manuku)

Geopelia striata

8" **WS** 11"

INTRODUCED

Introduced to Oʻahu in 1922, these diminutive doves are now ubiquitous across all of the main Hawaiian Islands. Also known as Barred Doves, they are found in urban and suburban habitats, where they search for seeds and insects in short grassy fields or for crumbs around outdoor restaurants. In courtship, males coo and bow to females as they show off their tails. The birds are susceptible to avian pox, which can result in a deformation of their feet. Their small size makes them easy to differentiate from Hawaiʻi's other common introduced dove species, the Spotted Dove. Vocalizations are appealing *coos* and a rapid, froglike, grating call.

Small, slender, pale brown dove. Gray head, bare blue skin around eyes. Back, wings, and breast heavily barred dark brown.

Mourning Dove (Manuku)

Zenaida macroura

L 11" | **WS** 17.5"

INTRODUCED

Familiar and abundant in North America, the Mourning Dove was introduced to Hawai'i Island in the 1960s. They have since been sighted on all of the main islands apart from Lāna'i, apparently dispersing naturally, but are uncommon and tend to be either geographically restricted or not fully established. Mourning Doves utilize a wide range of habitats but prefer open areas where they can gorge on seeds; they can store over ten thousand in their crop. These resourceful birds can also survive on brackish water. They have a mournful vocalization; the first portion is drawn out and rises sharply: *oooo-woo oooo ooo ooo*.

Slender, pale brown with pointed tail, light gray crown, nape, and breast. Blue-black patch on cheek, large dark spots on upper wing.

Mariana Swiftlet

Aerodramus bartschi

L 6" **WS** 10.5"

INTRODUCED, ENDANGERED

The Mariana Swiftlet is a native of the Mariana Islands. Up to 385 swiftlets were introduced to Oʻahu from Guam in 1962 and 1965. The Hawaiian birds ultimately became important for conservation after the brown tree snake arrived in Guam, decimating the original population. A small colony of Mariana Swiftlets still nests in an irrigation tunnel in Hālawa Valley, Oʻahu, and they can be seen catching insects above the ʻAiea Loop Trail. They create ingenious nests of vegetation glued to the wall and use echolocation to hunt insects, making a soft, staticky twitter sound.

Only swift in Hawaiian Islands. Small, dark gray-brown with paler throat, chest, and rump. Short, slightly forked tail.

Hawaiian Common Gallinule ('Alae 'ula)

Gallinula galeata sandvichensis

L 13" **WS** 21"

ENDEMIC SUBSPECIES, ENDANGERED (U.S.)

The 'Alae 'ula is an endemic subspecies of the Common Gallinule. Once widespread throughout the main Hawaiian Islands,
it is now restricted to Kaua'i and O'ahu, mainly due to introduced predators and habitat loss. The Hawaiian name, meaning
"burnt forehead," refers to the bright red frontal shield that
protects the gallinule's face from dense vegetation. In Hawaiian
folklore, these wetland birds are considered to be the "bringers
of fire." They have specially adapted toes (rather than webbed
feet) that help them cross floating vegetation and mudflats.
They skulk in dense vegetation or at the water's edge and build
well-hidden platform nests. Their call is a rapid, descending
quacking or random clucks.

Brown back, slate-gray
body, white side stripe.
Bright red frontal
shield, red bill with
yellow tip. Orange-
red legs and feet.

Hawaiian Coot ('Alae ke'oke'o)

Fulica alai

L 15" **WS** 25"

ENDEMIC, ENDANGERED

Found on all of the main islands except Kahoʻolawe, these endemic wetland birds number in the low thousands. Despite this, they are easy to see in a variety of human-created wetland habitats (such as golf courses) and natural wetlands, especially on Kauaʻi and Oʻahu. They have lobed feet that help them move efficiently in swampy areas and build nests of floating vegetation, where they lay up to 10 eggs. Research has found that coots make more interisland trips than Hawaiian Common Gallinules. Their travel is helping to preserve their genetic diversity. Their call is a repeated, high *kack*.

Chunky, slate-gray bird with white (occasionally red) frontal shield and white beak. Red eyes. Legs gray, with large lobed feet. Sexes alike.

Hawaiian Stilt (Aeʻo)

Himantopus mexicanus knudseni

L 14-15" | **WS** 28"

ENDEMIC SUBSPECIES, ENDANGERED

Look for these photogenic birds at mudflats, ponds, taro fields, even water-treatment plants on all of the main islands except for Kahoʻolawe. They are an endemic subspecies of the Black-necked Stilt. Maneuvering around wetlands on long, pink legs, the birds use their needle-like bills to catch a wide range of prey, including insects, fish, and crabs. Hawaiian Stilts are vulnerable to introduced predators such as cats, mongoose, rats, and bullfrogs. They nest close to water and use a broken-wing display to distract those predators from their young. Their call is a loud, excited, repetitive *kik kik*.

Slender black and white wader with very long pink legs and thin, black, needle-like bill.

Pacific Golden-Plover (Kolea)

Pluvialis fulva

L 9-10" | **WS** 17"

WINTER VISITOR

Like the humpback whale, the Pacific Golden-Plover is a harbinger of winter in Hawai'i. Locals look for its arrival in early fall and watch it leave in breeding plumage by April (although a small number stay year-round). Polynesian sailors are said to have followed it to Hawai'i, knowing that it must be heading to land. From breeding grounds in Alaska and Siberia, thousands of plovers navigate to the Hawaiian archipelago using the sun, stars, and the earth's magnetic field. They can be found fattening up for the return journey on lawns, golf courses, and meadows, from the coast right up to highland areas such as the crater of Maui's Haleakalā. In Hawaiian, their name is synonymous with "someone who leaves." Their call consists of a short, mournful whistle, upturned at end: *weet, kleep* or *pee-a-weet*.

Breeding plumage: black belly and head, with pure white line running from forehead down neck to breast. Golden back.

When seen flying inland at dusk, can be confused with inbound petrels, but smaller, stockier with shorter wings and rapid, direct flight.

Winter plumage: slender golden-brown bird with small head, thin black bill, and distinct pale brown eyebrow.

Black-bellied Plover

Pluvialis squatarola

L 11" **WS** 23"

WINTER VISITOR

Though much rarer than our wintering Pacific Golden-Plovers, Black-bellied Plovers turn up and overwinter in Hawaiʻi annually, and the same individuals are recorded in some locations year after year. The birds' ability to fly fast helps them complete their trans-Pacific journey. Look closely for this species among flocks of Pacific Golden-Plovers; they are very similar. The birds have large eyes, which they put to good use for nocturnal foraging. Outside of North America, they are referred to as Grey Plovers. Their call is a whistled *pee-a-wee*.

In non-breeding plumage, very similar to common Pacific Golden-Plover but slightly larger, with thicker bill and faint eyebrow.

Semipalmated Plover

Charadrius semipalmatus

L 7" | **WS** 14"

WINTER VISITOR

These migratory shorebirds are regular but uncommon visitors
to Hawai'i, passing over on their way from arctic North
America and occasionally overwintering on the main islands.
They are found on beaches, mudflats, and wetlands. Semipalmated Plovers run and pause when they feed, darting forward,
then stopping to probe for prey. The birds have short webbing
between the toes, hence the name "semipalmated" (they leave
tracks that can help with identification). It can be difficult to
differentiate Semipalmated Plovers in non-breeding plumage
from the Common Ringed Plover, which is a vagrant to the
islands. Vocalizations include a two-note whistle: *chu-eep*.

Non-breeding
plumage: white collar,
brown breast band,
diffuse white eye
stripe, white forehead,
black bill with orange
base, pale orange legs.

Bristle-thighed Curlew (Kioea)

Numenius tahitiensis

L 15-17" | **WS** 33"

WINTER VISITOR, VULNERABLE

A winter visitor to Hawai'i, the Bristle-thighed Curlew is the only shorebird whose migration is restricted to offshore islands in the tropical Pacific. It makes one of the longest non-stop flights over open ocean of any shorebird—2,500 miles from Alaska to the Northwestern Hawaiian Islands. Most migrants stop there, but some continue to the main islands. When present, they are relatively easy to spot on the north shore of O'ahu, in Kahuku and the James Campbell National Wildlife Refuge. No one knew where the Bristle-thighed Curlew bred until the 1940s, when nests were located in the tundra of western Alaska. The bird's curious name refers to the bare, shiny feather shafts on the thighs; their purpose is unknown. The curlew typically eats insects, crabs, and reptiles, but it is also known to snack on the eggs of seabirds. Its call is a whistling *ki-o-ea*, hence the Hawaiian name.

Large, bulky wader with long, curved, pink bill darker to tip. Pale gray legs.

O'ahu's north shore is a great place to look for this species. Search in fields and even graveyards.

Dark brown back, heavily speckled with tan. Pale brown eyebrow, brown eye stripe. Lightly streaked neck.

Ruddy Turnstone ('Akekeke)

Arenaria interpres

L 9.5"   **WS** 21"

WINTER VISITOR

One of our most common wintering waders, this stocky little species migrates through Hawai'i in spring and fall on its way to and from arctic breeding grounds. Ruddy Turnstones also overwinter in the main islands, and small numbers may remain over the summer. Typically found feeding in small flocks, they prefer shorelines, mudflats, fields, and grassy lawns. Turnstones are so named because they upend stones in their pursuit of prey, which includes insects and small fish. Most birds in Hawai'i wear their drab winter plumage, but early or late birds may be in their "ruddy" breeding plumage. The Hawaiian name reflects the call, a squeaky *a-ke-ke-ke*, or quiet whistles.

Small stocky shorebird with short dark bill and orange legs. In winter plumage, brown-gray above, white below, dark brown breast band.

Sharp-tailed Sandpiper

Calidris acuminata

L 8.5" | **WS** 18"

MIGRANT

Sharp-tailed Sandpipers breed mainly in Russia and winter in Southeast Asia and Australasia. They pass through Hawai'i on migration, particularly during fall, when they may show up on any of the main islands (although most records come from O'ahu and Maui) and the Northwestern Hawaiian Islands. A lone bird may overwinter occasionally, and they are also sometimes seen migrating back through Hawai'i in spring. Look for them in wetlands and mudflats. Migratory shorebirds are one of the pleasures of birding in Hawai'i, as they certainly pose a fun ID challenge. The Sharp-tailed Sandpiper's call is a repeated *weet weet*.

Medium-sized shorebird with chestnut cap, white eye stripe, short dark bill with olive base, yellow-olive legs. Breast lightly streaked.

Sanderling (Hunakai)

Calidris alba

L 8" | **WS** 17"

WINTER VISITOR

These winter visitors are common in Hawai'i, the majority arriving in August and leaving for the arctic tundra in April. Hunakai, their Hawaiian name, means "sea foam," and these little shorebirds are always one step away from the waves, darting forward and back as they look for invertebrates that the ocean leaves behind. Sanderlings will also feed on reefs in low tide, mudflats, even in flooded fields. While in Hawai'i, they often flock with other shorebirds but are easy to pick out, with their dancing movements and pale gray coloration. Their call is a twittering *quit* or *quit-quit*.

Small, fast-moving sandpiper. Very pale gray above, crisp white below. Short black bill, black legs.

Dunlin

Calidris alpina

L 8.5" | **WS** 17"

WINTER VISITOR

Dunlin are uncommon but regular winter visitors to Hawaiian shores as they make their way to and from breeding grounds in coastal tundra in the northernmost reaches of North America. Most birds that make it to the main islands overwinter, and there is evidence that the same individuals return in subsequent years. During this period, they can turn up on any of the main islands and like to hang out on mudflats, marshes, and beaches. They probe the mud with their long, sensitive bills in search of worms, mollusks, and crustaceans. Their call is a short, buzzy *chrreeet*.

Small gray wader with relatively long black bill, slightly downturned at end. Black legs and feet. Faint white eye stripe.

Least Sandpiper

Calidris minutilla

L 5-6"   **WS** 10.5-11"

WINTER VISITOR

Occasional winter visitors to the main Hawaiian Islands, these diminutive sandpipers breed throughout the tundra and boreal forest of North America and winter from Central America to northern South America. They are the smallest of the "peeps," weighing just one ounce. Look for them on mudflats or marshy areas, where they feed by grabbing prey at the surface or probing the mud for invertebrates and amphipods. The birds use the surface tension of the water to transfer prey quickly from bill tip to mouth. They often appear hunched as they creep along searching for food. Their call is a single high-pitched peep or a short trill.

Very small sandpiper with thin, slightly curved black beak and short yellow legs. Faint white eye stripe, lightly streaked breast.

Pectoral Sandpiper

Calidris melanotos

L 8-9" | **WS** 18"

MIGRANT

These tundra breeders come through Hawai'i on migration in fall as they head toward wintering grounds in central and southern South America. Males leave the breeding grounds in mid-summer; females and juveniles take flight a month or two later. The species rarely overwinters in the Hawaiian Islands. Pectoral Sandpipers can be found in a range of wetland areas, typically feeding in wet vegetation away from the water's edge. On their breeding grounds, they make an eerie, hooting *ooh ooh ooh* call, reminiscent of petrels; on their wintering grounds, calls are restricted to reedy, cheeping alarm calls.

Medium-sized sandpiper with streaked cap, white eye stripe, short dark bill, orange legs. Breast heavily streaked to white belly, forming contrasting "bib."

Long-billed Dowitcher

Limnodromus scolopaceus

L 11.5" | **WS** 19"

WINTER VISITOR

Long-billed Dowitchers breed in Siberia, Alaska, and Canada and overwinter in Hawai'i regularly, but in small numbers and relatively late in the year. These birds can be confused with the very similar Short-billed Dowitcher, which is a much rarer vagrant to Hawai'i. The two are best told apart by their calls, as the Long-billed's *keek* is higher-pitched than the Short-billed's *tu tu tu*. Long-billed Dowitchers' distinctive bill makes them stand out from the crowd, but they also feed with an unusual up-and-down "sewing machine" movement. They can be found in marshes, taro patches, and mudflats. *Limnodromus*, its genus name, means "marsh racer."

Large, heavy-set, gray sandpiper with white underparts, long dark bill with greenish base. Greenish legs. White back patch in flight.

Spotted Sandpiper

Actitis macularius

L 7.5" | **WS** 15"

VAGRANT

The Spotted Sandpiper may be the most widely distributed breeding sandpiper in the United States, but it is a vagrant to Hawaiʻi. It can turn up on any of the main islands in coastal areas and wetland habitats and can be identified by a fluttering flight and jerky run (hence its common nickname "teeter-peep"). It will eat almost any prey it can swallow, even catching insects from the air; it will sometimes swim; and it can dive to avoid predators. Its call is a piping *weet weet weet*, which may be extended when the bird is alarmed.

Small, active shorebird that bobs tail constantly. Heavily spotted breast and neck, but spots fade in winter. White eye stripe, pale legs.

Wandering Tattler ('Ūlili)

Tringa incana

L 11"   **WS** 26"

WINTER VISITOR

These slate gray waders are migrants and winter visitors, and a familiar feature along rocky shorelines on the main Hawaiian Islands. The birds arrive in mid-July and leave again by May for their Alaskan and Canadian streamside breeding grounds. A small number also stay on the islands over the summer. They are usually seen alone, hopping from rock to rock at the edge of the sea as they hunt for invertebrates. In Hawaiian folklore, tattlers are sentinels, sounding the alarm at intruders. Their call is reminiscent of their Hawaiian name, a high-pitched *oo-li-li-li*, often extended. This is perhaps the best way to tell them apart from the very rare Gray-tailed Tattler (*Tringa brevipes*), which is a vagrant to the Hawaiian Islands, and has a more mellow, whistled two or three toned call, upslurred at the end.

Non-breeding with slate-gray back, head, chest. Dark bill, partial white eye stripe and eye ring, dark gray lores. Bobs tail.

Lesser Yellowlegs

Tringa flavipes

L 10.5" **WS** 24"

MIGRANT, WINTER VISITOR

After breeding in boreal habitats in northwestern North America, Lesser Yellowlegs head south toward wintering grounds in the southern United States and Central and South America. They are regular visitors to Hawai'i during migration, though in very small numbers. Less than half of these slender sandpipers stay the whole winter, but a few transient birds might turn up in spring on the return journey. They are often confused with Greater Yellowlegs, which are significantly rarer in Hawai'i, but Lesser Yellowlegs are smaller and less bulky and have a shorter, straight bill. Their calls are a *tew* note, single, paired, or extended in alarm.

Slender shorebird with thin black bill and long yellow legs. Gray-brown upperparts, white underparts, light streaking on chest, barred tail.

Red Phalarope

Phalaropus fulicarius

L 8.5" **WS** 17"

WINTER VISITOR

Three phalarope species are recorded in Hawai'i, but only Red Phalaropes are observed regularly. Pelagic during the non-breeding season, they are seen mainly offshore in Hawaiian waters in March and April, although it is possible to observe them throughout winter. Swift, slender waders, they fly close to the water and swim in tight circles, tail erect, when looking for invertebrates on the surface. Bad weather can result in an influx of birds to coastal wetlands. Unfortunately, they are not in breeding plumage while here, so birdwatchers miss the intense coloration that gives the birds their name.

Winter plumage (shown): pale gray, not streaked, back; dark patch behind eye and short thick bill, pale yellow at base.

Pomarine Jaeger

Stercorarius pomarinus

L 18.5" | **WS** 52"

MIGRANT

The most common of the three jaeger species seen off Hawai'i, Pomarine Jaegers are recorded on pelagic trips and occasionally in coastal waters during winter, after they leave their arctic breeding grounds. Peak sightings occur from November through March. Formidable predators, they cruise the open ocean looking for smaller birds. Once they find a target, they pursue it relentlessly until it regurgitates, providing an easy meal (such piracy is known as kleptoparasitism). Jaegers will also forage for scraps from fishing boats. In their breeding grounds, they are entirely dependent on brown lemmings for food. Without a lemming irruption, many birds don't breed.

Adults with long, twisted, central tail feathers, dark brown upperparts, and pale black-tipped bill. Dark and light (shown) morphs.

Laughing Gull ('Opa'ipa'i)

Leucophaeus atricilla

L 16.5" | **WS** 40"

WINTER VISITOR

Surprisingly, very few gulls are seen in Hawaiian waters. The conditions might look perfect, but gulls generally need shallow water around continental shelves to feed; the remote, volcanic island dropoffs are unsuitable, and most gulls are vagrants. The Laughing Gull, however, is an almost annual winter visitor. Most are first-year birds that appear during migration from breeding grounds in Mexico, the Caribbean, or the Atlantic coast of North America. They can turn up on any of the main islands, where they can be found on the coast or over large water bodies.

In immature plumages, pale gray smudging on head, neck, and breast. White eye ring. Thick, dark bill, dark legs.

Ring-billed Gull ('Opa'ipa'i)

Larus delawarensis

17.5" | **WS** 48"

WINTER VISITOR

Ring-billed Gulls are one of the few gulls seen regularly in the main Hawaiian Islands. Typically first-year birds show up in small numbers in winter. Scavengers, they can be found on any island at sewage-treatment plants and garbage dumps but also along the coast and at wetlands. A widespread breeder in Canada and the northern United States, Ring-billeds were heavily persecuted in the early twentieth century, resulting in a massive population crash. They have since rebounded and are now common and familiar throughout their range.

In immature plumages, pale gray back, white head and chest with gray-brown streaking, pink legs, black-tipped pink bill.

Glaucous-winged Gull ('Opa'ipa'i)

Larus glaucescens

L 26" | **WS** 58"

WINTER VISITOR

Glaucous-winged Gulls are seen in the Northwestern Hawaiian Islands more often than on the main islands. Arriving in winter, these large visitors are presumably first-year birds that went off course slightly while migrating from Siberia and the northwestern coast of the United States to Japan and Baja California. Like Laughing Gulls, they eat what they can find, including refuse, carrion, and mollusks, dropping shells from the air to break them, and they can be aggressive, killing prey as large as a pigeon. They hybridize with other species, including Herring, Western, and Glaucous Gulls, making identification difficult.

Large bulky gull. First-winter birds pale gray, streaked with white. Primaries and back similar pale gray. Heavy, large, black bill, gray-pink legs.

Brown Noddy (Noio kōhā)

Anous stolidus pileatus

L 17" | **WS** 32"

NATIVE

Noddies are named for their habit of nodding to one another while nesting. Most Brown Noddy breeding colonies are found on the Northwestern Hawaiian Islands. These graceful native terns are also often seen around the main islands, particularly offshore, but breeding is restricted to Kaʻula and several offshore islets on Oʻahu. Eggs can be laid year-round, although the breeding season in the main islands peaks from March to October. Look out for this species among Black Noddy flocks, as well as in flocks of their own. They catch prey, usually squid and small fish, by hovering over the water. They are vocal within breeding colonies, issuing deep, grating caws and croaks.

Larger than Black Noddy, with thicker bill, brown body and tail, pale gray cap with white forehead, small black legs and feet.

Black Noddy (Noio)

Anous minutus

L 15" **WS** 30"

NATIVE, ENDEMIC SUBSPECIES

Two subspecies of this diminutive tern are found in the Hawaiian Islands: the orange-legged endemic *melanogenys* (known as the Hawaiian Noddy) and the dark-legged *marcusi* (found in the tropical northwestern Pacific). Colonial nesters, Black Noddies prefer offshore islets, caves, and cliff faces in the main Hawaiian Islands, where the Hawaiian Noddy is prevalent. In the Northwestern Hawaiian Islands, they construct more typical nests of sticks in naupaka and other shrubs. Birds can be seen feeding above schools of predatory fish, close to nesting sites, in coastal waters or brackish lagoons, rarely venturing far out to sea. Black Noddies make chattering and croaking calls, higher-pitched than Brown Noddy.

Smaller than Brown Noddy with dark chocolate body, grayish tail. Striking white cap, pale gray neck. Legs orange or black.

Blue-gray Noddy
Procelsterna cerulea saxatilis

L 10-11" **WS** 18-24"

NATIVE

Blue-gray Noddies prefer remote islets and breed throughout
the Pacific Ocean. In Hawai'i, they nest mainly in the Northwestern Hawaiian Islands, especially Nihoa and Necker. They
are capable of breeding year-round and stay close to their
breeding colonies. They may also nest on Ka'ula and have been
spotted around Kaua'i (including Lehua), but this species is
very difficult to see in the main islands. They tend to forage in
coastal waters around their breeding colonies year-round. Their
favored prey are larval fish, caught by dipping at the surface,
but they will also take crustaceans and insects. Around 3,600
breeding pairs live in the Hawaiian Islands. Calls at colonies
include a quavering *yeaaar* and squeaky chatters.

The world's smallest tern.
Blue-gray back, wings, and tail.
Primaries darker. Pale head, thin,
dark gray beak, and dark gray legs.

White Tern (Manu-O-Kū)

Gygis alba

L 11-13" | **WS** 27-34"

NATIVE

The native Manu-O-Kū (White or Fairy Tern) breeds throughout the Northwestern Hawaiian Islands. On the main islands, the species is restricted to Oʻahu, where its favored breeding grounds are in downtown Honolulu. A local phenomenon, it can be seen easily in city parks such as Kapiʻolani, Fort DeRussy, and ʻIolani Palace. Urban nesting began in 1961, when a pair nested on Koko Head. Now numbering around 2,000 individuals, the birds raise their young in such trees as monkeypod or banyan, laying a single egg in a fork or on a branch. Chicks use claws on their webbed feet to cling to the tree until a parent returns carrying small fish. White Terns shows little fear of humans and will even hover in their vicinity. They have a repetitive, harsh *eh-eh-eh-eh-yeh-yeh-yeh-yeh-yeh* call.

All white with short black bill with blue base, and pale gray legs and feet.

Only tern seen flying around Honolulu; easily identified by pure white plumage.

White Terns do not build any type of nest structure, instead laying their eggs in the forks of tree branches and other exposed areas.

Chicks are mix of pale brown, gray, and white and sit confidently on exposed branches, rocks and walls, secured by strong feet.

Sooty Tern ('Ewa'ewa)

Onychoprion fuscatus

L 16" | **WS** 32"

NATIVE

Native Sooty Terns are Hawai'i's most abundant breeding seabird, although the majority breed in the Northwestern Hawaiian Islands. In the main islands, there are breeding colonies on Ka'ula and on two islets off O'ahu. Sooty Terns form large, raucous, dense breeding colonies, often containing huge numbers of nests spaced evenly across open ground. The birds typically hover above feeding schools of tuna and other predatory fish and snatch the squid and fish that attempt to escape the frenzy below. Due to their noisy colonies and their calls, which include a raucous *wide-a-wake*, they are known as the "wide awake" bird.

Slender tern with black head, wings, and forked tail. White lores. Black legs. Underparts white.

Gray-backed Tern (Pākalakala)

Onychoprion lunatus

L 14-15" | **WS** 29-30"

NATIVE

The majority of the breeding population of this native tern is found on the Northwestern Hawaiian Islands, although the species also breeds on Moku Manu and Kaʻula in the main islands. The best chance of seeing it in the main islands is from Oʻahu or on a pelagic trip during the summer months. Relatively shy, the Gray-backed Tern tends to form small colonies in remote islands; consequently, relatively little is known about its habits. Prey consists of small fish at sea, but it also forages on terrestrial insects and even skinks. It can be confused with the more common and superficially similar Sooty Tern. Gray-backed Terns give high-pitched calls that sound like a squeaky dog toy.

Pale gray back, wings, and tail, white underparts. Contrasting black crown, nape, eye stripe. White eyebrow stripe. Black bill and legs.

Least Tern

Sternula antillarum

L 8.5"   **WS** 20"

NATIVE

Least Terns like to breed in open sandy areas, along river edges, and on sparsely vegetated islands in North America and the Caribbean. They winter in Central and South America. Most records in the main Hawaiian Islands are from May to October. Although the tern is uncommon in the islands, breeding has been confirmed on both Oʻahu and Hawaiʻi Island and also seems to have occurred on occasion on the Northwestern Hawaiian Islands. The smallest North American tern, this species has faced serious conservation challenges. Populations were decimated to provide feathers for women's hats in the late 1800s. Today, they suffer from disturbance in the breeding grounds.

Very small. Pale gray above, white below. Black cap, white forehead. Bill yellow when breeding, black at other times. Yellow legs, feet.

White-tailed Tropicbird (Koaʻeʻkea)

Phaethon lepturus dorotheae

L 30" | **WS** 37"

NATIVE

These elegant native seabirds are widespread throughout tropical and subtropical oceans, and their glorious tail streamers make them a Hawaiian favorite. Though very scarce on the Northwestern Hawaiian Islands, they breed throughout the main islands (apart from Niʻihau and Lehua). Half the Hawaiian population breeds on Kauaʻi, using cavities on steep cliffs; the birds can breed year-round. Their courtship displays and loud calls make them conspicuous. On Hawaiʻi Island, they are known as "crater birds" since they nest at the Kīlauea caldera despite the sulfurous fumes. They use their orange, serrated, dagger-like bills to catch flying fish and squid. In flight, they make loud, chattering, stuttering calls.

Slender white body and wings, long white tail streamers. V-shaped black lines on back, black leading edge to primaries.

Red-tailed Tropicbird (Koaʻeʻula)

Phaethon rubricauda

L 37" | **WS** 41"

NATIVE

Large populations of Red-tailed Tropicbirds breed across the Northwestern Hawaiian Islands. On the main islands, they are seen less frequently than the White-tailed Tropicbird, but populations may be increasing. The largest colonies are on Niʻihau, Kauaʻi, and Oʻahu. Red-tailed Tropicbirds are beautiful and graceful seabirds. During the breeding season, several pairs may take part in courtship displays that include circling, steep dives, and even flying backwards. Their serrated beaks help catch flying fish and squid. Their tail feathers were highly prized by Hawaiians for making kahili, or royal feather standards. Very vocal in flight, the birds make a variety of croaks, screeches, and chatters.

More heavyset than common White-tailed Tropicbird with all-white body and wings. Black patch on secondaries. Long red tail streamers.

Black-footed Albatross (Kaʻupu)

Phoebastria nigripes

L 32"   **WS** 84"

NATIVE, NEAR THREATENED

Black-footed Albatross breed primarily on the Northwestern Hawaiian Islands. Unlike Laysan Albatross, Black-foots are rarely seen on the main islands, although they can be spotted at sea occasionally during the breeding season (November to July), especially from Kauaʻi and Oʻahu. Their only breeding sites in the main islands are on Lehua and Kaʻula. The birds fly long distances to find food for their chicks, and they are adept at taking squid and fish from the surface. They also follow ships and can get snagged on the baited hooks used in longline fishing. Courtship displays center around head bowing and bill clacking; the birds' repertoire of vocalizations includes nasal brays, groans, and whistles.

Large, dusky gray albatross with powerful, white-edged dark gray bill. Black legs and feet.

Laysan Albatross (Mōlī)

Phoebastria immutabilis

L 32" | **WS** 78"

NATIVE, NEAR THREATENED

The majority of the breeding population of Laysan Albatross is found in the Northwestern Hawaiian Islands; Midway alone holds more than 400,000 pairs. Smaller populations exist on the main islands, including at Kaʻena Point on Oʻahu, and the birds are accessible to birdwatchers at multiple locations on Kauaʻi during the breeding season (November to July), even nesting in residential areas on the north shore. Once almost wiped out by feather collectors, Laysan Albatross have made a comeback, but longline fishing, introduced predators, and plastic ingestion still claim thousands. The species is known to be long-lived, and a female named Wisdom holds the world record for the oldest known bird. At 69 years old, she is still breeding. Laysans' beguiling courtship display includes at least 25 dance moves, and they have a wide range of vocalizations, including elaborate whistles, whinnies, honks, and bill clacks.

In flight, proportionally very long gray-brown wings, white head, breast, and rump, dark tail.

On ground, large and ungainly. White head with delicate dark gray around eye. Large pale pink-orange bill and pink feet.

Chicks covered in fluffy gray down; white breast feathers appear gradually after a few months.

Short-tailed Albatross

Phoebastria albatrus

L 36" | **WS** 87"

NATIVE, VULNERABLE

One of the rarest albatross species in the world, the Short-tailed Albatross currently numbers fewer than 2,000 pairs. In the 1800s, hunters destroyed every breeding colony but one, on Torishima Island in Japan. This was reduced to ten nesting pairs, almost driving the species to extinction. Since then, under intensive management, populations on four Japanese Islands have increased slowly. A social attraction project was initiated on Midway in the Northwestern Hawaiian Islands, and in 2010, breeding was confirmed. Several chicks have since fledged. A female-female pair on Kure has laid eggs, but they were unfertilized. The birds include bowing and vocalizations such as grunts, moans, and bill clacks in their mating dance. These beautiful, multi-coloured albatross are the largest of the three albatross species breeding in the Hawaiian Islands.

Large. White with golden head and neck. Dark wings with white patch. Pink bill, blue tip. Immatures have brown nape and cap.

Kermadec Petrel

Pterodroma neglecta

L 15" | **WS** 36"

MIGRANT

Looking like a cross between a falcon and a seabird, these large gadfly petrels breed mainly on islands in the South Pacific, including the Kermadec Islands in New Zealand. They are seen occasionally on pelagic trips from Hawai'i during fall and winter. Intriguingly, several birds have been observed in summer around Kilauea Point National Wildlife Refuge on Kaua'i (one between 1998 and 2000 and up to three from 2011 to the present day). There they can be seen with relative ease as they harass incoming boobies and shearwaters until they give up their food. This piracy is known as 'kleptoparasitism' and is one of their main foraging techniques, although they also hunt squid and fish which they take from the surface. It is possible that the Kilauea birds may be breeding, although this has not been confirmed. Kermadec Petrels utter strange calls, including a rising and falling "car alarm" scream during flight.

Large stocky petrel with pale flashes under primaries. Two morphs: dark (shown) is gray-brown; light has variable amount of white on head, underparts.

Hawaiian Petrel ('Ua'u)

Pterodroma sandwichensis

L 16" | **WS** 37"

ENDEMIC, ENDANGERED

Hawaiian Petrels were once one of the most abundant species on this island chain. Their bones have been found in large numbers at archaeological sites, including numerous coastal areas. Collisions with powerlines, introduced predators (cats, mongoose, rats, pigs), light attraction, and habitat loss, have all combined to reduce their population dramatically. Now they breed only in inaccessible mountain areas, nesting in burrows in lush native forests and barren volcanic landscapes. The main breeding concentrations are on Kaua'i, Lāna'i, and Maui; each population is genetically different. The breeding season extends from February to December, with birds breeding a month earlier on Maui than Kaua'i. A pelagic trip is a good way to see Hawaiian Petrels during this time, but they can also be spotted from shore at dusk as they fly inland toward their colonies under the cover of darkness. There they make mournful *uuuu-ah-uuuuuu* calls, coupled with squeaks and chatters.

In flight, long gray wings and back, white belly, and distinctive white forehead, best seen when bird approaches head-on.

Flight style includes high, smooth arcs above ocean with few flaps, different than shearwaters.

Nests in deep burrows in mountainous areas. Gray back and tail, white forehead, strong dark gray bill.

Bonin Petrel

Pterodroma hypoleuca

L 12"   **WS** 25-28"

NATIVE

Although Bonin Petrels once bred on the main islands, they currently breed only in the Northwestern Hawaiian Islands, making them the Pacific's most northerly breeding gadfly petrel. Unlike most other shearwaters and petrels in Hawai'i, which breed during the summer, these native birds arrive at their colonies in late July and breed in winter. Rat eradication has been vital for the recovery of populations on Midway and Kure, and birds from the Northwestern Hawaiian Islands are being translocated to the James Campbell National Wildlife Refuge on O'ahu as part of a reintroduction program begun in 2018. A pelagic species, Bonin Petrels are rarely seen at sea close to the main islands. They make varied calls, including squeaks, churrs, squeals, and moans.

Diminutive petrel with soft pale gray plumage. White forehead lightly speckled with pale gray. Gray beak and feet.

Black-winged Petrel

Pterodroma nigripennis

L 12" | **WS** 26"

MIGRANT

Black-winged Petrels breed in large numbers on islands in the southwestern Pacific. Up to three million pairs nest on Macauley Island (in the Kermadec Islands), making them one of the most numerous New Zealand seabirds. In Hawaiian waters, they are frequently seen during their northern migrations, mainly from April to October. These birds can be spotted during pelagic trips during the right time of year but are rarely seen from shore; they prefer to forage over deep water, capturing small crustaceans and squid from the surface. They feed at night and by day.

Small petrel with pale gray upperparts and white underparts. Dark eye patch. Distinctive wide black line on underwings.

Bulwer's Petrel ('Ou)

Bulweria bulwerii

L 10-11" | **WS** 30-35"

NATIVE

These small native petrels do not dig a burrow but lay a single egg in a rock cavity or pile, on a ledge, or under vegetation. They are fairly common breeders in the Northwestern Hawaiian Islands, but predation (particularly by rats and cats) has restricted them to a handful of small offshore islets in the main islands. Cryptic and enigmatic, Bulwer's Petrels are best seen at sea, typically singly and often on the outskirts of flocks of other foraging seabirds or near pods of cetaceans. They feed on fish, squid, and crustaceans. While silent at sea, they utter prolonged soft barking noises in their colonies.

Bulwer's Petrel are capable of nesting in very tight crevices and small holes. Small brown petrel with proportionally long wings and tail. Usually seen singly. Paler chin stands out in good light. Seen here with False Killer Whale.

Sooty Shearwater

Ardenna grisea

L 17" | **WS** 40"

MIGRANT, NEAR THREATENED

Sooty Shearwaters breed on southern islands near Australia, New Zealand, and South America and disperse afterward throughout global waters. Common migrants in Hawaiian waters, they are most often seen at sea in March and April and from September to November, although they can be present at other times of the year. The best chance of spotting them is on a pelagic trip, but it is worth scanning from coastal watchpoints as well. Masters of migration, Sooty Shearwaters are known for their epic journeys. Some birds travel an incredible 40,000 miles a year.

Medium-sized brown shearwater with short tail and large silvery patches on underwings. Often seen migrating in numbers.

Wedge-tailed Shearwater ('Ua'u kani)

Ardenna pacifica

L 16-18" | **WS** 38-41"

NATIVE

This is one of the most abundant breeding seabirds in Hawai'i. Wedge-tailed Shearwaters nest in large colonies on the Northwestern Hawaiian Islands and the main islands, laying their eggs in burrows made in sand, soil, or rock piles along the coastline. The birds return in March and remain until December. Easy to spot at protected areas like Kīlauea Point National Wildlife Refuge on Kaua'i, they are also visible from shore, particularly in the late afternoon as they gather at sea before returning to their colonies after dark. The birds target small fish fleeing from large predatory fish such as tuna; this habit helps lead fishermen to their catch. While common, Wedge-tailed Shearwaters are vulnerable to introduced predators (especially cats and dogs), and newly fledged birds can be attracted to artificial lights and become grounded, unable to return to the air. The birds are very vocal at colonies, making distinctive, eerie, moaning cries.

Two morphs. More common light morph (shown) has pale gray back and tail, multi-toned. Belly white, grayish sides.

Dark morph with slate-gray upper- and underparts.

Long wedge-shaped tail. Flies low over water, flapping infrequently. Often in large groups.

Christmas Shearwater

Puffinus nativitatis

L 14-15"   **WS** 28-32"

NATIVE

This dark-colored native shearwater is named after Kiritimati (formerly Christmas Island). It is a relatively common breeder on the Northwestern Hawaiian Islands, with a stronghold on Laysan, but it breeds on only a handful of offshore islets in the main islands, including Kauʻula, Moku Manu, and possibly Lehua. Christmas Shearwaters arrive in February and depart Hawaiian waters by November. The best chance to see them in the main Hawaiian Islands is on a pelagic trip. Typical flight patterns involve long glides and rapid wingbeats. Vocal in colonies, the birds utter worried, honking *oh*'s, like a ball slowly bouncing.

Small shearwater with entirely chocolate-brown plumage. Slender black bill. Flies with rapid wingbeats, usually seen singly.

Newell's Shearwater ('A'o)

Puffinus newelli

L 13" | **WS** 8.7-9.8"

ENDEMIC, ENDANGERED

Once numerous, this species was thought to be extinct until a grounded bird was found on O'ahu in 1954 and a colony subsequently discovered on Kaua'i in 1967. The bird faces numerous threats, including powerline collisions, light attraction, and introduced predators, but management actions are attempting to reverse its decline. The Newell's Shearwater nests in burrows beneath ferns or tree roots in dense forest and on steep slopes and cliffs, principally on Kaua'i, and moves to and from the breeding grounds only at night. It flies with rapid wingbeats, low over the water, and has a distinctive "braying donkey" call, usually heard only in or near colonies.

Medium-sized shearwater. Black upperparts, crisp white underparts. White flanks extend into "thumbprint" behind each wing.

Nests in deep burrows in mountainous areas, although a small coastal population can be found at Kīlauea Point National Wildlife Refuge on Kaua'i.

Leach's Storm-Petrel

Oceanodroma leucorhoa leucorhoa

L 8" | **WS** 19"

MIGRANT

Leach's Storm-Petrels are distributed throughout the Northern
Hemisphere, breeding on islands throughout the North Atlantic
and North Pacific. The birds disperse widely in winter and are
usually recorded in Hawaiian waters from October to April.
Seen on pelagic trips during this period, they can be easily
confused with the Band-rumped Storm-Petrel, which breeds
in Hawai'i, since the Leach's deeply forked tail can be hard to
see. Leach's Storm-Petrels take zooplankton and plankton
from the ocean surface while hovering and pattering with
their feet. They are sometimes attracted to the bright lights
of cruise ships.

Brown storm-petrel with
forked tail, large white
rump patch, and broad pale
band across upper wing.

Band-rumped Storm-Petrel ('Ake'ake)

Oceanodroma castro

L 8" | **WS** 19"

NATIVE, ENDANGERED

The endangered Band-rumped Storm-Petrel is an enigmatic seabird, both scarce and cryptic in nature. It breeds on remote islands in the Atlantic and Pacific, and recent genetic work suggests multiple subspecies within this distribution. Until the discovery in 2017 of burrows on Hawai'i Island, nesting sites were unknown in the Hawaiian archipelago. There is also evidence of breeding on Lehua, Kaua'i, and Maui. The best chance of seeing this species is on a pelagic trip during the breeding season, from May to mid-November. At colonies, the storm-petrel's squeaky call sounds like a wet finger on the edge of a wine glass.

Dark brown storm-petrel with white rump and short, dark, square tail. Normally seen singly. Patters over water's surface when feeding.

Tristram's Storm-Petrel

Oceanodroma tristrami

L 7-8" | **WS** 17-18"

NATIVE, NEAR THREATENED

Tristram's Storm-Petrel is a winter breeder (October to May) in the Northwestern Hawaiian Islands and on islands off Japan. The Hawaiian population is estimated to be around 6,000 pairs. Although a translocation project initiated in 2018 promises to establish a breeding colony at the James Campbell National Wildlife Refuge on Oʻahu, sightings in the main islands are very rare and occur mainly on pelagic trips around Kauaʻi. Tristram's Storm-Petrels feed by snatching prey from the surface of the ocean; they sometimes patter with their feet. At colonies, they have a squeaky, bouncy call that gets progressively faster.

Chocolate-brown with deeply forked tail and brown rump. Broad pale band across upper wing.

Great Frigatebird ('Iwa)

Fregata minor palmerstoni

L 34-40" **WS** 81-91"

NATIVE

Frigatebirds cast a long shadow over seabird colonies, and not just because of their huge wingspan. Although they can catch prey from the surface of the water, one of their main feeding techniques is to harass other seabirds, pulling at their feathers until they regurgitate (the Hawaiian name 'Iwa means "thief"). Frigates breed almost exclusively on the Northwestern Hawaiian Islands, apart from a few errant breeding records, but the main islands host multiple roosts where the birds can be seen with relative ease. They are generally quiet except at colonies, where they make a wide range of screeches, quavering warbles, and whinnies.

Large, with long angular wings, forked tail. Adult male all black, red throat pouch. Adult female (inset) with white throat and breast.

Masked Booby ('Ā)

Sula dactylatra personata

L 32" | **WS** 62"

NATIVE

Masked Boobies are the largest and rarest of the three boobies in Hawai'i. Most of the breeding population lives on the Northwestern Hawaiian Islands. In the main islands, breeding is restricted to Ka'ula and Moku Manu, and birds are seen occasionally offshore, mainly from Kaua'i and O'ahu. Masked Boobies are ground nesters, breeding from January to July. They lay two eggs. If both hatch, the first chick typically throws the second out of the nest (a reproductive strategy called siblicide). Boobies plunge-dive from up to 100 feet to catch fish and squid. Females utter a croak or honk, males a high whistle.

Large white booby with black wings and tail. Striking yellow eyes, black mask, yellow or bone-colored beak, brighter in male.

Brown Booby ('Ā)

Sula leucogaster plotus

L 30" | **WS** 57"

NATIVE

A very widespread species, Brown Boobies are found in warm waters across the world, including the Pacific, Atlantic and Caribbean. They are seen year-round in the waters of the main Hawaiian Islands, especially near Kaua'i and O'ahu. The largest colonies are on Ka'ula, Lehua, and Moku Manu and on Nihoa in the Northwestern Hawaiian Islands. The birds are often found within 50 miles of land in mixed feeding flocks following schools of predatory fish as they force prey to the surface. Boobies fold back their wings and plunge like feathered javelins, remaining underwater for up to 40 seconds. At colonies, their calls consist of wheezing whistles (males) and croaks or honks (females). They are easily identifiable from the other booby species in the Hawaiian Islands by their predominantly brown plumage. Juveniles look similar to adults but have a dirty brown belly instead of the crisp white of adults.

Brown head, neck, wings, and body. White chest. Large yellow feet. Flush on face blue on male (left), yellow on female (right).

Red-footed Booby ('Ā)

Sula sula

L 28" | **WS** 60"

NATIVE

Red-footed Boobies are common in Hawaiian waters. Breeding
colonies in the main islands are found on Ka'ula, Lehua, and
O'ahu, and the birds at Kīlauea Point National Wildlife Reserve
on Kaua'i (the largest colony) are easy to see. Boobies can also
be spotted from almost any coastal location on Kaua'i and
O'ahu, as they often fly in small groups just offshore. Sightings
of birds offshore are much less common in the other main
islands. Red-footed Boobies feed in association with schools of
predatory fish like tuna, plunge-diving after prey that the tuna
drive to the surface. The birds also follow boats and sometimes
even land on them. While plumage varies across the species'
wide tropical range, Hawaiian birds are typically light morphs,
although the occasional dark morph can be seen. They are very
vocal in their colonies, uttering varied sounds, including hoarse
croaks, chattering, and guttural honking.

White-morph
adults all white with
black primaries and
secondaries. Pale
blue bill with pink
flush to surrounding
skin. Red feet.

In flight, black primaries and secondaries contrast sharply with all white body and head. White tail helps differentiate from Masked Booby.

Juvenile pale gray, darker around head and wings. Off-white belly. Pale pink feet.

Cattle Egret

Bubulcus ibis

L 20"　**WS** 36"

INTRODUCED

Start up a lawn mower anywhere in the Hawaiian Islands, and a Cattle Egret will probably appear within a few minutes to munch up disturbed insects. Originally from Africa and Asia, these birds have become established on every continent but Antarctica, often following humans as they cleared land for agriculture. They were introduced to the main Hawaiian Islands in 1959 as biocontrol agents to reduce insects plaguing cattle, but they have become pests themselves, predating the eggs and chicks of native waterbirds and seabirds. Control efforts have had limited effect. The birds utter a raspy, monotonous *hwark*.

Breeding plumage (shown): buff crown, nape, back, and breast, reddish pink legs, orange bill. Non-breeding: all white, Yellow bill, black legs.

Black-crowned Night-Heron ('Auku'u)

Nycticorax nycticorax hoactli

L 23-26" **WS** 45-46"

NATIVE

This is Hawai'i's only native heron. Black-crowned Night-Herons usually inhabit large wetlands across the main Hawaiian Islands and are vagrants to the Northwestern Hawaiian Islands. Most active at dusk, night, and dawn, the birds stand motionless, waiting for prey to come within range before lunging with their sharp beak. Some crafty birds have even learned to "fish," throwing bait to lure their prey closer. Night-herons fly slowly, with steady wingbeats. Juvenile birds look different from adults and are sometimes mistaken for other species. The call is a hoarse *kwak*, often uttered when flying.

Adult (shown) pale gray with black back and crown. Bright red eye, dark bill. Juvenile gray brown, heavily streaked.

White-faced Ibis
Plegadis chihi

L 23" | **WS** 36"

VAGRANT

These charismatic vagrants make it to Hawai'i occasionally, much to the delight of birders. They can turn up on any of the main Hawaiian Islands. Most sightings are of juveniles. The birds arrive alone or in small groups in fall, and some individuals have stayed for years. They like extremely shallow water such as marshes and flooded fields, where they probe for insects in the soft mud or eat aquatic plants. They will also take frogs and fish. Young birds could be confused with the Glossy Ibis, which has not been confirmed in Hawai'i yet.

Juvenile (shown) brown with slender streaked neck, long downward-curved dark bill. Wings and back metallic green. Adults maroon with white around bill.

Osprey (Osepera/'Okepela)

Pandion haliaetus

L 23" | **WS** 63"

WINTER VISITOR

Found almost worldwide, Osprey visit the main Hawaiian Islands nearly every year. Some overwinter, and there are occasional reports of birds in the summer. They are usually seen watching over ponds, river mouths, and other water bodies or cruising for fish along the coast. They dive on their piscine prey, hitting the water feet-first, then lift off with a fish held firmly in their massive talons. If you see a large bird of prey flying with slow wingbeats over or near water in the main Hawaiian Islands (excluding the 'Io), it is most likely an Osprey. These migrants can fly over 150,000 miles during their lifetime.

Gray-brown above, white below. Striking yellow eyes, powerful hooked bill, gray-brown eye stripe. In flight, long, slightly bent wings.

ʻIo (Hawaiian Hawk)

Buteo solitarius

L 16-18" | **WS** 34-40"

ENDEMIC, NEAR THREATENED

The ʻIo is one of two endemic birds of prey on the Hawaiian Islands. (The other is the Hawaiian Short-eared Owl.) Formerly found on Oʻahu, Molokaʻi, Kauaʻi, and Hawaiʻi Island, the ʻIo is now restricted to Hawaiʻi Island for reasons that remain a mystery. The population is estimated to be around 3,000 individuals, yet the hawk is a relatively common sight over agricultural or forested areas. These expert hunters prey on rats, insects, and other birds. They nest in a jumble of twigs and sticks in a tree, and pairs protect their territory throughout the year. Light and dark morphs appear in roughly equal numbers. Majestic raptors, ʻIo are symbols of Hawaiian royalty and are also considered to be ʻaumākua (spirit guides). They utter a variety of calls, including a screeching *ʻio*, like their Hawaiian name.

Dark morph with chocolate-brown plumage, lighter brown underparts. Black beak, yellow legs and feet. Female larger than male.

Light morph with gray-brown wings, back, and head. Underparts white with brown streaking on chest. Female larger than male.

In flight, small head, chunky body, short wide tail, short broad wings. Soars frequently.

Pueo
(Hawaiian Short-eared Owl)

Asio flammeus sandwichensis

L 13-17" | **WS** 33-41"

ENDEMIC SUBSPECIES

One look at a Pueo, an endemic subspecies of Short-eared Owl, will explain why Hawaiians consider it to be an 'aumakua (spirit guide). It has huge, haunting yellow eyes and is often seen hunting birds, insects, and rodents in dramatic locations such as the cliffs of the Waimea Canyon on Kaua'i. Since the owl is primarily diurnal and crepuscular, there is a good chance of spotting it in daylight. The fossil record suggests it appeared after the arrival of the Polynesians, perhaps because they introduced rats. Hawaiian Short-eared Owls nest year-round, laying up to six eggs on the ground in a shallow depression lined with grass and down. Displaying males ascend by flying in small circles and then hang in the wind before clapping their wings while stooping. Collisions with vehicles, loss of habitat, and poisoning are causing populations to decline across the islands. Pueo make a cat-like *ree-yow*, short barks, and a hooting courtship song.

Large dark brown owl with pale brown flecking to back and pale brown barring to tail. Shows ear tufts when alert.

In flight, noticeably long dark brown wings with pale barring on primaries and secondaries. Frequently flies during day.

Prominent pale facial disc, striking yellow eyes, dark brown around eyes. Pale breast streaked dark brown.

Barn Owl
Tyto alba

L 16"   **WS** 42"

INTRODUCED

The presence of Barn Owls in Hawai'i demonstrates what happens when humans tinker with nature. Introduced in the 1950s by the Hawai'i Department of Agriculture to control rats in sugarcane fields on Kaua'i, O'ahu, and Hawai'i Island, the owls rapidly moved on to depredate native seabirds, particularly small species such as the Black Noddy and Bulwer's Petrel, and are now common throughout the main islands. Unlike the Hawaiian Short-eared Owl (Pueo), which is seen frequently during the day, Barn Owls are mainly nocturnal. Their eerie shriek has led to legends in which Barn Owls figure as harbingers of death.

Pale brown and silvery gray with heart-shaped white facial disc. In flight, white underparts make owl look very pale.

Peregrine Falcon
Falco peregrinus

L 16" **WS** 41"

WINTER VISITOR

There are very few raptors in the Hawaiian Islands, but this migratory falcon puts in a regular appearance, as single birds arrive each fall and often overwinter. The fastest bird in the world, the Peregrine Falcon can reach staggering speeds of over 200 mph when it dives for prey. Not a picky eater, it will take bats, rodents, and a wide assortment of birds, including such endangered species as the Laysan Duck and Laysan Finch in the Northwestern Hawaiian Islands. This varied diet accounts for the falcon's global distribution. Four subspecies have been reported from the islands. Peregrines make loud, repetitive calls: *cak cak cak*.

Large solid-looking raptor. Slate-gray back, dark mustache, heavily barred belly. In flight, broad pointed wings, short tail. Juvenile gray-brown.

Rose-ringed Parakeet

Psittacula krameri

L 16" | **WS** 18.5"

INTRODUCED

Originally from sub-Saharan Africa and India, the introduced Rose-ringed Parakeet has made itself at home in Hawai'i, which has no native parrots. Able to survive in a range of habitats and climates, escapees from the pet trade have proliferated across the world. Since the first invaders are thought to have escaped from a bed-and-breakfast on Kaua'i in the 1960s, the population increase on that island has been staggering. Efforts are now underway on Kaua'i to control this species. The invasive parakeets are now established on O'ahu and have been sighted on Maui and Hawai'i Island. They damage commercial fruit crops and form large noisy flocks in residential areas.

Large green parakeet with long tail. Heavy red beak, black throat, and rose-edged neck band. Raucous.

'Alalā (Hawaiian Crow)

Corvus hawaiiensis

L 19-20"   **WS** 36-42"

ENDEMIC, ONCE EXTINCT IN THE WILD (RECENTLY REINTRODUCED)

The 'Alalā is restricted to Hawai'i Island and is the last survivor of five Hawaiian crow species. Habitat destruction, disease, illegal shooting, and introduced predators caused the population to crash, and by 2002 the last wild pair vanished from South Kona. Luckily, a group of Hawaiian Crows had been brought into captive-breeding facilities in the late 1970s, saving the species from extinction. The 'Alalā Project, an effort to re-establish a wild population, commenced releasing birds in 2016. Three years later, several pairs were finally observed nesting, an important milestone on the long road to recovery. Omnivorous, social, and intelligent, the crow is an important distributor of native seeds, and it will also eat the eggs and nestlings of other birds. Hawaiians consider it an 'aumakua (spirit guide). 'Alalā are very vocal; their repertoire of calls includes mournful whistles, growls, and bizarre human-like screams

Large all-black crow. Thick, heavy, black bill with bristle-like feathers at base. In flight, fan-shaped tail.

'Alalā are color-banded. If you see one, report band combinations to 'Alalā Project.

Kaua'i 'Elepaio

Chasiempis sclateri

L 5.5" | **WS** 7-8"

ENDEMIC, VULNERABLE

There is one endemic species of 'Elepaio on Kaua'i, another on Hawai'i Island, and a third on O'ahu. Each was afforded full species status in 2010. In the past, the range of the vulnerable Kaua'i 'Elepaio included lowland forested areas down to the coast, but the birds are restricted to upper montane areas today. They are confiding little flycatchers, relatively easy to see in Kōke'e, especially on the Pihea Trail and Alaka'i Swamp Trail. They use all levels of the canopy, hanging upside-down while catching insects and spiders and even hopping on the ground. The birds occupy the same territory annually and weave dense cup nests from lichen and moss. They are vulnerable to predation by rats and cats but may have some immunity to avian malaria, unlike many of the honeycreepers. 'Elepaio call regularly, especially at dawn and dusk, and make a wolf whistle, a scolding, squeaky, machine-gun song, and a whistled *pai-o* or *ele-pai-o*.

Typical adults pale gray above with white wingbars and white rump. Ochre and brown throat and breast. Sexes alike.

Coloration can vary; some birds mixed brown and gray, particularly when grading from juvenile to adult plumage.

Juvenile brown with orange-brown wash to head, throat, and breast. Orange-brown wingbars. Yellow base to lower half of bill.

O'ahu 'Elepaio

Chasiempis ibidis

L 5.5" | **WS** 7.5"

ENDEMIC, ENDANGERED

The endangered O'ahu 'Elepaio was once ubiquitous on O'ahu but began a precipitous decline in the 1970s due to rat predation, avian malaria, and other causes. In 2012, the population was estimated to include fewer than 1,200 individuals. Rat control is key to the species' conservation. These confiding and long-lived birds (the oldest banded bird was over 22 years old) are now restricted to fragmented areas in the Wai'anae and Ko'olau Mountains and are difficult to see. The 'Aiea Loop Trail may yield sightings. Their whistled song mirrors their name: *ele-pai-o*.

Adults brown above with white wingbars and white rump. Throat typically black (male), black-flecked white (female shown with young).

Hawai'i 'Elepaio
Chasiempis sandwichensis

L 5.5" | **WS** 7.5"

ENDEMIC, VULNERABLE

This versatile species can be found in higher elevations across
Hawai'i Island. They have three regional plumage variations
that are so remarkably different that some authorities had even
considered them to be subspecies. These are *bryani*, found in
dry high elevations on the western slope of Maunakea; *ridg-
wayi*, observed in warmer wet forests in eastern Hawai'i; and
sandwichensis, seen in drier forests on the western side of the
island. Recent research, however, suggests they should not be
considered subspecies. Hawaiians regard this bird, like all
'Elepaio, as an 'aumakua (spirit guide). Its name comes from its
song: *ele-pai-o.*

Three plumage types,
varying substantially in
white on head and
chest. Maunakea birds
typically have most
white on head.

Eurasian Skylark

Alauda arvensis

L 7"   **WS** 12-14"

INTRODUCED, VAGRANT

Settlers homesick for the extended song of the Eurasian
Skylark introduced the bird to the main Hawaiian Islands
from Europe or Asia in the mid-1800s. The lark belts out its
melody as it flies high in the air, continues as it makes a
graceful spiraling descent, and stops only when it drops to the
ground. Skylarks were soon found on most of the main islands,
although their status on Kaua'i is now uncertain and their
range has contracted on O'ahu. They prefer open grasslands
and fields. Occasionally, vagrant skylarks from a migratory
Asian population arrive on the islands, although only a few
confirmed records exist.

Small pale brown bird,
heavily streaked darker
brown. Pale eye stripe. May
raise streaked crown feathers
into crest when alert.

Red-vented Bulbul

Pycnonotus cafer

L 8.5" | **WS** 10-11"

INTRODUCED

Red-vented Bulbuls were brought from India and Southeast Asia to O'ahu as cage birds but escaped in the mid-1960s and rapidly colonized the island. Now they are common in urban and forest areas, where they perch in conspicuous exposed locations and utter short, scratchy calls. They have been reported on the other main islands, but swift efforts have been made to remove them, as they are considered an agricultural pest. You can help by reporting sightings outside O'ahu to the Hawaii Invasive Species Council at 643pest.org. Red-vented Bulbuls utter a range of mechanical chirps and whistles, including a three-tone *chee-chury-chur.*

Dark brown back, wings, and tail. Black-brown head, feathers often raised into crest. Bright red under tail. White-tipped tail.

Red-whiskered Bulbul

Pycnonotus jocosus

L 8" | **WS** 11"

INTRODUCED

Of the two bulbul species found on Oʻahu, Red-whiskered is less common. Native to Southeast Asia, it was introduced as a cage bird and subsequently escaped or was released. Now it can be seen in urban areas as well as valleys and forests. Red-whiskered Bulbuls are conspicuous and noisy, not shy. Not only are they an agricultural pest, but they also spread the seeds of invasive plants, so efforts are underway to keep the birds from dispersing to other islands. Report sightings outside Oʻahu to the Hawaiʻi Invasive Species Council at 643pest.org. Their call is a distinctive, whistled *sweet-doo-di-do*.

Brown upperparts, pure white underparts. Black head, prominent long black crest. Pale red under tail. White cheek, red patch behind eyes.

Japanese Bush-Warbler

Horornis diphone

L 5.5" **WS** 8"

INTRODUCED

You might not see a Japanese Bush-Warbler in Hawai'i, but you will almost certainly hear one. It tends to skulk in the undergrowth but utters a loud and explosive whistling call reminiscent of its Japanese name, Uguisu, along with short, "kissing" calls. The bird was introduced on O'ahu from 1929 to 1941 to control insects and quickly dispersed to all the main islands. It can be found everywhere, from urban lawns in the lowlands to native rainforest in the mountains. Japanese Bush-Warblers likely compete for food with native species. In Japan, they are known as harbingers of spring.

Nondescript, small, gray-brown bird with pale gray and white underparts. Faint white eyebrow, pale gray eye stripe.

Japanese (Warbling) White-eye

Zosterops japonicus

L 4"   **WS** 6-7"

INTRODUCED

If you see a small green bird flitting through the bushes in the garden of your home or hotel, it is almost certainly a Japanese White-eye. This diminutive songbird is one of the most common birds in Hawai'i and found in most habitats. Introduced from Japan from 1920 to 1930, it spread rapidly across all the islands. Unfortunately, the species is a carrier of avian malaria. The disease is deadly for native forest birds, but the white-eye itself is resistant. The bird's presence may have helped spread the mosquito-borne illness, threatening endangered native species. Japanese White-eyes utter a rambling, high-pitched, whistling song and short calls and chitters.

Small, bright green bird, yellower on head and throat. Prominent white eye ring. Pale gray belly.

Greater Necklaced Laughingthrush

Garrulax pectoralis

L 13" | **WS** 16-17"

INTRODUCED

This introduced Asian babbler is present only on Kaua'i, where it has been established for around 100 years. A secretive, skulking species, it remains difficult to see and is sparsely distributed, primarily in the east and north of the island, in lowland forests, near streams. Birds have been reported around the Hulē'ia National Wildlife Refuge, on Sleeping Giant, and above Kalāheo, as well as at higher elevations such as the Alaka'i. Greater Necklaced Laughingthrushes are fond of fruit, especially papaya and banana. More often heard than seen, they give loud, fluting whistles that often descend in tone and varied harsh or rattling calls.

Large thrush-like bird. Brown upperparts, black-bordered white cheek, black necklace sometimes bordered blue-gray. Rufous sides, off-white throat and chest.

Melodious Laughingthrush

Garrulax canorus

L 10" | **WS** 14-15"

INTRODUCED

Legend has it that the Melodious Laughingthrush (or Chinese Hwamei) was introduced when birds were freed from cages during a severe fire in Honolulu's Chinatown in 1900. Following the colonization of Oʻahu, the laughingthrushes were introduced to Kauaʻi, Maui, and Hawaiʻi Island, where they became common. Their presence on Lānaʻi and Molokaʻi is uncertain. It is difficult to get a good look at these birds, as they skulk in vegetation; they are more easily found by their vocalizations. Although they are called melodious, their long song is generally harsher and more rasping than that of the White-rumped Shama and Northern Mockingbird.

Brown with orange cast to forehead and thighs. Large white eye ring extends in streak down neck. Yellow beak.

Red-billed Leiothrix

Leiothrix lutea

L 5.5" | **WS** 6.5-7.5"

INTRODUCED

Native to Southeast Asia, this colorful little bird was introduced to most of the main Hawaiian Islands (except Lāna'i) in
the early 1900s. You can still find them on O'ahu, Maui, Hawai'i
Island, and Moloka'i, but they have inexplicably disappeared
from Kaua'i. (The last sighting was in 1977.) This was the first
species in Hawai'i to be documented with avian malaria.
Red-billed Leiothrixes prefer mid- to high-elevation native
rainforest and exotic forest habitats with thick understories.
The birds form small flocks and are easier to see than hear;
listen for their melodic refrains and chattering call.

Small pale gray bird with
bright red bill, orange-
yellow throat, and bright
orange-yellow edges on
primaries. Olive forehead.

Millerbird (Ulūlu)

Acrocephalus familiaris

L 5"

ENDEMIC, CRITICALLY ENDANGERED

The critically endangered Millerbird was once found on both Laysan and Nihoa in the Northwestern Hawaiian Islands. The Laysan subspecies was driven to extinction in 1923 by introduced rabbits that destroyed the island's vegetation, depriving the birds of food and shelter. Over 100 birds remain in the Nihoa population. After extensive restoration work, 50 Millerbirds were re-introduced to Laysan in 2011–12. (The species received its new Hawaiian name Ulūlu at the same time.) The new arrivals soon started nesting, and the population has expanded. Millerbirds' song is a short warble, metallic in nature.

Dark brown with pale brown underparts and white throat. Pale eye stripe. May raise crown feathers into short crest.

White-rumped Shama
Copsychus malabaricus

L 10" | **WS** 10-12"

INTRODUCED

Elegant White-rumped Shamas are found throughout Asia.
Introduced to Kaua'i in 1931 and O'ahu in the late 1930s, they
have since become established on Moloka'i and Lāna'i, and they
have also been recorded on Maui. They can be found in a wide
range of habitats, from gardens to native forests. Urban birds
may become relatively tame and will even follow gardeners in
the hope of snatching a disturbed insect. They have a loud,
melodious, bubbly song and are also excellent mimics. Listen
for their electrified tick-tick call, which separates them from
the Melodious Laughingthrush and Northern Mockingbird.

Male (shown) with metallic blue head, back, wings, and long tail. Orange underparts. Female and juvenile gray-brown with orange underparts.

ʻŌmaʻo

Myadestes obscurus

L 7ʺ | **WS** 8-9ʺ

ENDEMIC, VULNERABLE

The ʻŌmaʻo is a vulnerable endemic thrush found only on Hawaiʻi Island. It was first noted by Captain Cook's crew in 1779. Present in montane forests and other habitats on southern and eastern slopes above 3,000 feet, ʻŌmaʻo are relatively easy to find in Hawaiʻi Volcanoes National Park. They eat fruit or seeds, often perching motionless for extended periods after feeding. In the past, each main island had at least one thrush; only the ʻŌmaʻo and Kauaʻi's Puaiohi remain. The ʻŌmaʻo population is in decline, partly due to introduced predators. Songs involve varied, sweet, slurry notes, with short pauses.

Medium-sized plump thrush. Brown upperparts, pale gray underparts. Dark gray bill and legs. Sexes alike, juvenile heavily speckled.

Puaiohi
(Small Kaua'i Thrush)

Myadestes palmeri

L 6.5" | **WS** 10"

ENDEMIC, CRITICALLY ENDANGERED

This delicate, critically endangered thrush is endemic to Kaua'i. Once thought extinct, it was rediscovered in the 1960s. Today, the entire population, about 500 birds, is restricted to 12 square miles in the Alaka'i Wilderness Preserve. They nest in cavities or on shelves in rock walls created by stream erosion and usually draped with *Sadleria* ferns. Puaiohi are frugivores, and important dispersers of native seeds. They show signs of resistance to avian malaria but are vulnerable to rat predation. Their song is a short series of high, squeezed whistles, usually in four of five syllables: *pu-ai-o-hi*.

Slender thrush. Brown upperparts, pale gray underparts. Dark gray bill, pale legs. Off-white eye ring, dark throat stripe. Juvenile heavily speckled.

Northern Mockingbird

Mimus polyglottos

L 9" | **WS** 13"

INTRODUCED

The Northern Mockingbird will be familiar to many visitors from North America. It was introduced to Hawai'i in 1928 for pest control and aesthetic reasons and subsequently spread to all the main islands, where it can now be found in dry, scrubby areas. Mockingbirds eat a varied diet of insects, seeds, fruit, and the eggs or hatchlings of other birds. Named for an ability to imitate other species, the bird includes the vocalizations of the White-rumped Shama and Melodious Laughingthrush in its repertoire in Hawai'i. Individuals also make up their own songs and sing for long periods from exposed perches. Call is a harsh *chek*.

Slender, pale gray bird with whitish underparts. Long tail. White wingbars. Yellow eye, dark gray eye stripe.

Common Myna
(Piha'ekelo/Manu'aipilau)
Acridotheres tristis

L 10" | **WS** 47-55"

INTRODUCED

Everywhere you go in Hawai'i, you will come across Common Mynas scolding you and everything else around them. One of the 100 most invasive species in the world, they were brought to the islands in 1865 to control an infestation of armyworms in sugarcane plantations but rapidly became agricultural pests themselves. Worse, they prey on the eggs of native birds. Unusual for an introduced species, the Common Myna's omnivorous appetite and pugnacious personality have earned it several Hawaiian names that translate to "noisy" and "trash-eating bird." Very vocal, mynas announce their presence with a range of raucous calls.

Brown. Glossy black head and chest. Bright yellow bare facial skin, beak, and legs. In flight, white patches on wing.

Common Waxbill

Estrilda astrild

L 4" **WS** 5"

INTRODUCED

These natives of southern Africa multiplied rapidly after being introduced to Oʻahu in the 1970s. By the turn of the century, they had become one of the most common landbirds, and they recently became established on Hawaiʻi Island and Maui, most likely making the interisland ocean crossing unassisted as the population on Oʻahu expanded. There have also been sporadic sightings on most of the other main islands. Common Waxbills' diet consists mainly of grass seeds, so the birds are usually seen on the ground, often in urban areas. They utter high-pitched, bouncy chips in flight and short buzzy trills.

Small, pale gray-brown bird, finely barred across most of body. Bright red bill and mask, darker under tail, gray legs.

Lavender Waxbill

Estrilda caerulescens

L 4.5"   **WS** 8-9"

INTRODUCED

These pretty little finches originated in Africa and were introduced to both Oʻahu and Hawaiʻi Island. On Oʻahu, they are restricted to the southeast, where they have slowly declined and are now difficult to see, if they remain at all. They are present in low numbers on Hawaiʻi Island, mainly on the west coast. There were also sightings for a while on Maui (presumably from another introduction), but the birds have not been reported recently. These flocking birds prefer areas of dry, open woodland or brush where they feed mainly on insects and seeds. Their song is thin and squeaky.

Small, pale gray bird with rusty red tail and rump. Thin black eye stripe, rusty red bill, dark gray legs.

Orange-cheeked Waxbill
Estrilda melpoda

L 4.5" | **WS** 6.5-7.5"

INTRODUCED

These African natives were introduced to Oʻahu and Maui in the 1960s. They survived on Oʻahu until around 2014 and are now presumed extirpated. They are still present in small numbers on Maui, where they prefer dry grassland or brush in the center of the island. They search for seeds in flocks and are very acrobatic, climbing grass stems and hanging upside-down in their pursuit of food. Males perform a courtship dance while holding a stem in their bill. Orange-cheeked Waxbills can be confused with the superficially similar Common Waxbill. The Orange-cheeked's song is high-pitched and jingling.

Small, pale gray bird with brown back, rusty red rump, and orange cheeks. Bright red bill, gray legs.

Red Avadavat

Amandava amandava

L 4.5" | **WS** 4.5-5.5"

INTRODUCED

Originally from Asia, attractive Red Avadavats, or "Strawberry Finches," were introduced to O'ahu in the early 1900s, probably as cage birds. They appear to have dispersed naturally to Hawai'i Island, Kaua'i, and Maui (although they eventually disappeared from Maui). They are usually seen in small flocks searching for seeds in agricultural areas or grasslands near water. In the breeding season, males perform a courtship dance in which they bow to females while clasping a feather or grass stem in their bill. Red Avadavats make a *pseep* call in flight and a high-pitched whistled song.

Small, bright red with brown back and wings. Liberally spotted white. White crescent under eye, red bill. Females gray-brown with red rump.

African Silverbill

Euodice cantans

L 4" | **WS** 8"

INTRODUCED

Originally from sub-Saharan Africa, diminutive African Silverbills were introduced to Hawai'i Island in the late 1960s, and the island remains a stronghold. The birds subsequently dispersed in a northerly direction, colonizing each island in order, presumably through natural dispersal, and they have even occupied dry islets such as Lehua. African Silverbills are found most often in large flocks searching for seeds in fields, grassland or scrub, and thorn areas. Although they prefer dry habitats, they need a nearby water source. They make a *tik tik* call and have a short, trilling song.

Small, pale brown bird with white underparts. Dark brown primaries and tail. Pale blue eye ring, metallic blue bill, pale legs.

Java Sparrow

Lonchura oryzivora

L 6" | **WS** 8.5"

INTRODUCED, ENDANGERED

Trapping for the cage-bird industry has made the attractive Java Sparrow endangered in its home range of Indonesia, where populations have dwindled to a few thousand individuals. It proliferated after its introduction to Oʻahu in the 1960s, spreading naturally to the other main islands. Java Sparrows typically live in the vicinity of humans. Known as "rice birds," they feed on seeds and have been associated with agricultural losses and the spread of weeds. Their contact calls are stuttering twitters and chips.

Small, chunky, pale gray bird with black head, white cheeks, red eye ring, and pinkish bill. Pinkish gray belly, pale pink legs.

Scaly-breasted Munia
Lonchura punctulata

L 4.5" | **WS** 8-10"

INTRODUCED

An early introduction, this diminutive finch was brought to
Oʻahu from Asia in 1866. Now it is widespread and abundant on
all the main Hawaiian Islands. Previously known as "Nutmeg
Mannikins," Scaly-breasted Munias are usually seen around
fields and parks, although they can sometimes be spotted in
forests and at elevations up to 8,000 feet. They flick their tail
and wings regularly and are fond of grass seeds and crops. Culls
around airports or to protect rice paddies have had only
temporary success. Flocks can be very vocal, with a mix of
buzzy twitters and *chees*.

Small, pale brown bird
with dark brown throat,
dark gray beak, pale gray
legs. Distinctive scale
pattern on pale chest.

Chestnut Munia

Lonchura atricapilla

L 4.3-4.7" | **WS** 4-6"

INTRODUCED

A native of Asia, this stocky little bird appeared on Oʻahu in 1959, possibly as an escaped cage bird. It became well established on Oʻahu, Kauaʻi, and Maui and has also been sighted on the other main islands. Usually found in fields or grassy areas, Chestnut Munias will land on stalks of grass and work their way to the end to eat the seeds. They can be quite acrobatic, dangling upside down and contorting themselves to reach particularly tasty seeds. They tend to flock, often in large numbers. Call consists of high, plaintive *cheeps* and *pleeps*, which often give them away. They build small domed nests in tall grasses, bushes or trees and can lay up to 7 eggs.

Small, chestnut-colored bird with black head, throat, and breast. Prominent silvery bill. Sexes alike. Juvenile pale brown and tan.

House Sparrow (Manu liʻiliʻi)
Passer domesticus

L 6" | **WS** 7.5-10"

INTRODUCED

This very familiar species hails from Europe and the Middle East but has spread around the globe courtesy of humans. It came to Oʻahu via New Zealand in 1871 (although there may have been a previous introduction in 1859) and rapidly made itself at home. Content to eat almost anything, House Sparrows are now abundant throughout the main Hawaiian Islands. There is evidence that their isolation on the islands has caused rapid evolution, leading the Hawaiian sparrows to differ in plumage and size from their ancestors. Easily seen in urban areas, they make repetitive chirping and chipping noises.

Male with brown upperparts, gray underparts, chestnut cap, black on throat andlores.

Females and juveniles with pale brown head, eye stripe.

ʻAkikiki

Oreomystis bairdi

L 5" | **WS** 6-7"

ENDEMIC, CRITICALLY ENDANGERED

The ʻAkikiki is an energetic endemic honeycreeper that performs elaborate courtship dances and forages like a nuthatch, running along tree branches in pursuit of insects. Almost always, it is found in pairs or family groups, and its favored feeding and nesting locations include large ʻōhiʻa trees, but it is almost impossible to see in the wild. Having suffered a catastrophic decline over the last three decades caused by avian malaria and loss of breeding habitat from hurricanes, it is now critically endangered, restricted to 15 square miles of the Alakaʻi Wilderness Preserve on Kauaʻi. Its song is a short trill, heard so rarely that the bird is functionally songless.

Dark gray head, back, and flanks, contrasting with off-white throat and underparts. Short, slightly decurved, pink and gray bill.

Maui ʻAlauahio (Maui Creeper)

Paroreomyza montana

L 4.5"

ENDEMIC, ENDANGERED

This endangered endemic honeycreeper was once found on both Lānaʻi and Maui. While the Lānaʻi subspecies went extinct in the 1930s, the Maui subspecies is still relatively common in native forest and tree plantations, but its range has contracted to East Maui. The inquisitive nature of Maui ʻAlauahio makes them relatively easy to see. Look for them at Hosmer's Grove in Haleakalā National Park or Polipoli Springs State Recreation Area. They feed by foraging for insects in the understory, flicking up lichen and vegetation. Vocalizations include *chip* or *check* calls and also a sweet, short, whistled song.

Male (shown) bright yellow and olive-green. Female gray-green with yellowish tinge to head. Bill dark gray, short, and only slightly decurved.

Palila

Loxioides bailleui

L 7.5" **WS** 8-9"

ENDEMIC, CRITICALLY ENDANGERED

The critically endangered Palila is the last finch-billed honeycreeper in the main Hawaiian Islands. The fossil record shows it was on Kaua'i and O'ahu, but today it occurs on Hawai'i Island only, confined to just 25 square miles of dry, native forest on the western slope of Maunakea where sheep grazing has degraded the habitat and māmane and naio trees predominate. Ninety percent of its diet is māmane seeds and buds. The Palila Forest Discovery Trail is a good place to look for the birds. Their song is a lengthy, jumbled series of squeaky twitters, and trills that the Hawaiians considered a sign that rain was coming.

Bright yellow head and breast, gray back, pale gray underparts. Olive-green wings and tail. Female less vibrant.

Laysan Finch (ʻAinohu kauo)

Telespiza cantans

L 6.5" | **WS** 12-13"

ENDEMIC, VULNERABLE

The Laysan Finch is a finch-billed honeycreeper, like the Nihoa
Finch and Palila. Endemic to Laysan in the Northwestern
Hawaiian Islands, it was once abundant, but introduced rabbits
destroyed the bird's habitat, causing serious population
declines, so it was introduced to nearby Pearl and Hermes Atoll.
The Laysan Finch eats seeds, carrion, and seabird eggs; such
variety is thought to have helped it survive the rabbit scourge.
(The mammals were finally removed in 1923.) The biggest
threat today is sea-level rise caused by climate change. The bird
is a vocal virtuoso, with a long, twittering song.

Male (shown) with bright
yellow head and breast,
gray collar, olive-brown
upperparts. Female same
color pattern but paler,
with dark spots on back.

Nihoa Finch

Telespiza ultima

L 6"

ENDEMIC, CRITICALLY ENDANGERED

The critically endangered Nihoa Finch is omnivorous and intensely curious; it eats seeds, flowers, fruits, insects, and bird eggs, and it will explore researchers' belongings without fear. The fossil record shows that it once lived on the main Hawaiian Islands, but today it is present only on Nihoa, where its population numbers in the low thousands. In 1967, researchers tried to translocate birds to the French Frigate Shoals, the largest atoll in the Northwestern Hawaiian Islands. The attempt failed, but translocation was identified as a key conservation tool for protecting birds in the future. The Nihoa Finch has an unhurried, musical song that includes twitters, whistles, and trills.

Male (shown) with yellow head, breast, wings, and tail, pale gray back and tail. Female same color pattern but heavily streaked.

'Ākohekohe
(Crested Honeycreeper)

Palmeria dolei

L 7" | **WS** 9-10"

ENDEMIC, CRITICALLY ENDANGERED

This large, critically endangered honeycreeper is found only in East Maui, in wet forest above 5,000 feet on the slopes of Haleakalā. Its spectacular pom-pom-like crest helps to pollinate the trees and plants that the bird depends on for survival. Primarily nectivorous (although it will eat insects) and very territorial, it will chase off any birds that encroach on its nectar sources. The species was once present on Moloka'i, but disease, predation, and habitat loss due to cattle ranching resulted in extinction there; the last birds were seen in 1907. 'Ākohekohe are susceptible to introduced diseases; the high altitude of their current stronghold keeps them above mosquitos that spread avian malaria. Fewer than 2,000 birds remain in the wild, and breeding in captivity has had limited success to date. The honeycreeper makes a wide range of loud croaky calls, with upward whistles.

Large, slate-gray honeycreeper with prominent pale gray crest.

Orange-red eye ring and nape, speckled back, wings, and underparts. Dark gray underparts streaked pale gray.

Long gray legs allow birds to run between blossoms, sometimes doing acrobatics to reach flowers.

'Apapane

Himatione sanguinea

L 5" | **WS** 5-5.5"

ENDEMIC

'Apapane bring a dash of color to birding in Hawai'i. The birds depend largely on 'ōhi'a trees, flitting from bloom to bloom to take nectar with their brush-like tongues and leaving with a dusting of pollen on their faces. They are common in 'ōhi'a habitat over 3,000 feet on Kaua'i, Maui, and Hawai'i Island, but they are becoming uncommon on O'ahu and rare on Moloka'i, and they have been extirpated on Lāna'i.

'Apapane range for miles looking for fresh blooms and can often be seen flying over treetops. This leaves them vulnerable to avian malaria, since they can be exposed to mosquitos in lower-altitude forests. 'Apapane were important to ancient Hawaiians; the birds supplied feathers for royal capes and are woven into many stories. Their wings make a distinctive whirring sound, while their varied calls, which differ between islands, include staccato whistles, squeaks, trills, and chattering noises.

Bright red honeycreeper with black wings and tail and white under tail. Black, thin, decurved bill and black legs. Sexes alike.

Listen out for the distinctive song of the 'Apapane. Birds often sing from the tops of trees and exposed branches.

Juvenile plumage is patchy mix of olive, gray, and red, progressively gaining more red as bird transitions to adult plumage.

I'iwi

Drepanis coccinea

L 6" | **WS** 7-8"

ENDEMIC, VULNERABLE

I'iwi are not as easy to track down as 'Apapane, but these beautiful birds are well worth finding. They were once common across the main Hawaiian Islands, but their strongholds now are in high-altitude native forests on Hawai'i Island and Maui. They are becoming rarer on Kaua'i, are almost gone on Moloka'i, may be extinct on O'ahu, and are extinct on Lāna'i. Predation by rats and cats has played a role, but their decline is largely due to a susceptibility to avian malaria, which is exacerbated by the birds' tendency to search for blooming 'ōhi'a trees in the lowlands, where they encounter mosquitos. I'iwi use their curved bill to feed on the nectar from 'ōhi'a or māmane tree blossoms; insects feature in their diet, too. The honey-creeper appears consistently in Hawaiian folklore and chants, and hundreds of thousands of its feathers were used to create intricate featherwork items. Its song sounds like a high-pitched rusty swing.

Bright red, chunky honeycreeper with black wings and tail. Heavily decurved reddish orange bill and red legs.

Can be differentiated from superficially similar 'Apapane by bill shape and color, plumper body, and lack of white under tail.

Juvenile patchy gray and red with yellowish head; neck and back heavily speckled with pale gray.

Kiwikiu (Maui Parrotbill)

Pseudonestor xanthophrys

L 5.5" | **WS** 6.5-7.5"

ENDEMIC, CRITICALLY ENDANGERED

This critically endangered honeycreeper uses its hooked beak to expose insects, especially larvae, and mimics parrots in its gymnastic movements. Endemic to Maui but present only in East Maui, it is restricted to forests on the windward sides of Haleakalā. The Nature Conservancy's Waikamoi Preserve is the place to see it, but access is by guided hike only and must be arranged in advance. The population numbers in the very low hundreds. The Kiwikiu was thought to be extinct until the 1950s, and the first nest with eggs was not found until 1993. It received its present Hawaiian name in 2010, as the original had been lost. Conservationists are working to protect the Kiwikiu from a range of threats, and a captive-bred population has been created. Unfortunately, plans to translocate birds to the leeward side of Haleakalā suffered a severe setback in 2019 when most of the birds died from avian malaria. Its song is a short, high-pitched, downward-inflected trill.

Plump honeycreeper with olive-brown crown, back, wings, and tail. Bright yellow eye stripe, cheeks, and throat, dull yellow underparts.

Heavy bill; longer upper half curves over shorter, thicker, lower half.

Juvenile similar to adults but much paler, with plumage mixed with gray.

ʻAkiapōlāʻau
Hemignathus wilsoni

L 5.5" | **WS** 7-8"

ENDEMIC, ENDANGERED

The endangered ʻAkiapōlāʻau is found only on Hawaiʻi Island, where approximately 1,900 birds remain in isolated high-elevation forest. The Hakalau Forest National Wildlife Refuge and Puʻu ʻŌʻō Trail are strongholds. The ʻAkiapōlāʻau's bill is an evolutionary marvel; the lower half allows the bird to drill into tree trunks like a woodpecker for sap or insects, while the extended upper half operates like a hook to extract the food. Fledglings remain with their parents for an extended period to get the hang of working their multipurpose beak. The Hawaiian name means "hammerhead." The song is a short musical refrain, sometimes ending in a trill.

Upper half of bill extended and heavily decurved. Male (shown) with bright yellow head, olive-green upperparts. Female grayish olive with yellow throat.

'Anianiau

Magumma parva

L 4" | **WS** 6-7"

ENDEMIC, VULNERABLE

This tiny bird weighs a third of an ounce and is the smallest Hawaiian honeycreeper. Nectivorous 'Anianiau use a tube-like brushy tongue to feed on 'ōhi'a blooms, and they also pierce flowers with their bill to sip nectar and take insects. Their Hawaiian name means "straight-beaked." Found only on Kaua'i, the species has suffered population declines due to avian malaria, habitat loss, and predation, but patient birdwatchers can still find it on the Alaka'i Swamp Trail or the Pihea Trail in Kōke'e. Its song is a sweet refrain that has been likened to a miniature sewing machine.

Male (shown) bright yellow and olive-green. Female duller yellow-green. Bill pinkish gray, short, and only slightly decurved. Pinkish gray legs.

Hawai'i 'Amakihi

Chlorodrepanis virens

L 4.3" | **WS** 6.5-7.5"

ENDEMIC

The Hawai'i 'Amakihi is found on Hawai'i Island, Mau'i, and
Moloka'i but is now extinct on Lāna'i. It eats nectar, insects,
fruit pulp, and tree sap and is usually found in 'ōhi'a forest.
Hosmer's Grove in Haleakalā National Park (Maui) or the Palila
Discovery Trail (Hawai'i Island) are good places to see it. This
bird may be developing resistance to avian malaria, as it is still
found at lower elevations than other native honeycreepers.
'Amakihi pierce native Lobelia flowers at the base to steal their
nectar. Its song is a rapid-fire trill, usually repeated.

Male (shown) bright
yellow-green with
black lores and thin,
slightly decurved, and
pale gray bill. Female
and juvenile grayer
with pale yellow tinge.

O'ahu 'Amakihi

Chlorodrepanis flavus

L 4.3" | **WS** 6-7"

ENDEMIC, VULNERABLE

O'ahu 'Amakihi are similar to the closely related Kaua'i and Hawai'i 'Amakihi in behavior and diet. They eat primarily nectar, insects, and fruit and pollinate native plants with their decurved bills, but they also steal nectar by piercing flowers near the base. The birds frequent 'ōhi'a forest but seem to be surviving in non-native forests at lower elevation than other native birds. This suggests that the O'ahu 'Amakihi may be developing resistance to avian malaria, allowing it to forage in areas where mosquitos are prevalent. The 'Aiea Loop Trail is a good place to see it. The song is a rapid-fire trill, usually repeated.

Male (shown) olive-green, dark gray lores and thin, slightly decurved, and pale gray bill. Female and juvenile grayer with pale olive tinge.

Kaua'i 'Amakihi

Chlorodrepanis stejnegeri

L 4.5" | **WS** 6.5-7.5"

ENDEMIC, VULNERABLE

Found only on Kaua'i, this species is larger than the Hawai'i and O'ahu 'Amakihi. It occurs in higher-elevation native forests containing 'ōhi'a and koa trees and can be observed flipping upside-down as it searches for insects hidden in bark. Since the Kauai'i 'Amakihi is declining, it is speculated that it is not developing resistance to avian malaria in the way that the O'ahu and Hawai'i 'Amakihi may be. Nonetheless, it is still relatively common in the Alaka'i Swamp and surrounding trails. Its song is a short, sweet, rapid-fire trill, first note higher.

Male (shown) olive-green, dark gray lores and thin, slightly curved, and pale gray bill. Female and juvenile grayer with pale olive tinge.

Hawai'i Creeper ('Alawī)

Loxops mana

L 4.5" | **WS** 6-7"

ENDEMIC, ENDANGERED

Hawai'i Creepers are found in four separate locations on
Hawai'i Island, all over 5,000 feet and dominated by 'ōhi'a and
koa trees. Chances of seeing them are decent at the Hakalau
Forest National Wildlife Reserve (currently accessible only with
a permitted guide), but the birds are relatively inconspicuous
and can be mistaken for several other species, so look closely.
Hawai'i Creepers eat mainly spiders and insects that they glean
from branches, moving up and down trunks like a treecreeper.
The Hawaiian name 'Alawī had been thought lost but was
rediscovered in 2017. The song is a quavering, descending trill.

Male (shown) olive-green,
female gray-green. Pale
throat, contrasting with belly,
dark lores and short, pale, and
only slightly decurved bill.

ʻAkekeʻe

Loxops caeruleirostris

L 4.5" | **WS** 6.5"

ENDEMIC, CRITICALLY ENDANGERED

Reminiscent of crossbills and similar to the Hawaiʻi ʻĀkepa, the tips of the ʻAkekeʻe's bill are offset. The adaptation helps the bird dig into ʻōhiʻa buds in their hunt for insects. Once present across Kauaʻi, ʻAkekeʻe are now restricted to less than 30 square miles of high-elevation forest in the Alakaʻi Plateau. The population is less than 1,000 individuals, so they are extremely difficult to see. Nonetheless, birds are occasionally spotted high in the canopy along the Alakaʻi Swamp Trail. The song is a soft trill that plateaus and then descends. The call is a short, upward cheep.

Small, greenish yellow honeycreeper with distinctive black mask. Short pale bill with offset bill tips. Long, thin, forked tail distinctive in flight.

Hawai'i 'Ākepa

Loxops coccineus

L 4" | **WS** 6"

ENDEMIC, ENDANGERED

A Hawai'i Island endemic, the Hawai'i 'Ākepa has an unusual bill. The lower half bends left or right, so its tip crosses the tip of the upper half. This helps the bird extract insects from 'ōhi'a leaf buds and koa leaves, usually high in the canopy. The Hakalau Forest National Wildlife Refuge is home to around half of the population; the remainder is in the Ka'ū Forest Reserve area. The related O'ahu 'Ākepa is extinct, and the Maui 'Ākepa, last seen in 1988, is presumed extinct, a victim of disease, introduced predators, and habitat loss. The Hawai'i 'Ākepa's song is a short, bouncy, descending trill.

Male (shown) bright orange with short pale bill and dark gray legs. Female with pale gray head, olive back, pale orange underparts.

House Finch (Ainikana)

Haemorhous mexicanus

L 6" | **WS** 8.5"

INTRODUCED

All of Hawai'i's native honeycreepers evolved from a common ancestor in a process known as adaptive radiation. It is thought that a finch species similar to the House Finch (possibly one of the rosefinches from Eurasia) may have been that ancestor. Whatever the case, the House Finch apparently was absent when Europeans arrived and was introduced to the main Hawaiian Islands in the mid-1800s. It can now be found on all islands. The Hawaiian name means "papaya eater." The bird's wide vocal repertoire includes buzzing calls and jumbled whistled or scratchy songs. Males also carry out a flight song.

Male (shown) with bright red (rarely yellow) head, throat, and breast. Brown upperparts, white underparts streaked brown. Female and juvenile lack red.

Yellow-fronted Canary

Crithagra mozambicus

L 4.5" | **WS** 8-9"

INTRODUCED

Common in Africa, this attractive finch was introduced to
O'ahu and Hawai'i Island in the 1960s, when cage birds were
deliberately released. It has also been reported recently on
Maui. Yellow-fronted Canaries can be confused with yellowish
House Finches, so pay careful attention to diagnostic features.
The canaries prefer parkland and wooded areas, where they are
seen in flocks, pecking at seeds and insects on the ground. They
can be difficult to spot in tall vegetation, but you might hear
them; they have a loud pleasant song, hence their alternative
name "Green Singing Finch."

Olive-brown upperparts, bright yellow
underparts. Head yellow with gray
crown and black throat stripe. Female
less bright, head pattern less defined.

Western Meadowlark

Sturnella neglecta

L 8-9.5"   **WS** 16"

INTRODUCED

Western Meadowlarks were released on most of the main
Hawaiian Islands in the early twentieth century, but most
of the introductions failed. They now persist only on Kaua'i,
where they can be found hunting for insects in fields. The
birds' powerful bill allows them to create holes in the soil
or in vegetation to get to grubs. Meadowlarks are ground
nesters, and young birds usually leave the nest before they
can fly. They are also avid songsters; males sing from exposed
branches or posts. Listen for their loud sweet songs uttered
in short refrains.

Pale brown with bright yellow
throat and breast, black necklace,
and eye stripe. Thick white eyebrow
yellow toward bill. Sexes similar.

Northern Cardinal

Cardinalis cardinalis

L 8-9" | **WS** 10-12"

INTRODUCED

Familiar to visitors from North America, the Northern Cardinal was introduced in 1929 when a caged bird escaped on Oʻahu; later, deliberate introductions followed. The bird is now an avian fixture in gardens and forests across the main islands. Both sexes are territorial and will aggressively repel intruders, even attacking their own reflections in car mirrors. Despite this, up to 35 percent of nestlings belong to a father other than the one feeding it. To maintain their red plumage, the birds' diet must include carotenoids from fruit and insects. A vocal species, they produce sweet, whistled, repetitive songs, and their contact calls are high-pitched *tics*.

Male bright red with black face and throat, heavy red bill. Crest. Female (inset) gray-brown with dull red crest and wings.

Red-crested Cardinal

Paroaria coronata

L 7.5" **WS** 11"

INTRODUCED

Originally from South America, these attractive birds were introduced to Kaua'i and O'ahu between 1928 and 1931, and they spread naturally to the other main islands. While common on most islands, they remain sparse on Hawai'i Island, where they may be outcompeted by the Yellow-billed Cardinal. Red-cresteds eat seeds and insects, usually feeding in pairs. During the breeding season, males are aggressive and will chase off potential interlopers. Males will also select a nest site and weave the cup-shaped nest. The quality of their work attracts females. Red-crested Cardinals make a squeaky contact call; their song has repeated, rising and falling, whistled notes. They also sing a scratchy duet.

Pale gray upperparts, white neck and underparts. Bright red head and crest, pale gray beak. Juvenile with orange-brown head.

Yellow-billed Cardinal

Paroaria capitata

L 7" **WS** 9-10"

INTRODUCED

This species was introduced to Hawai'i Island from South America in the 1960s. Initially recorded on the Kona Coast, Yellow-billed Cardinals swiftly expanded their range and can now be found throughout the island. They have not been recorded on any other main island. The birds prefer dry, scrubby areas and kiawe thickets in coastal zones but can also be seen hopping around urban centers looking for food. They resemble the Red-crested Cardinal closely, so beware of misidentification. Both species are in the tanager family, rather than the cardinal family. The Yellow-billed Cardinal's song consists of a lengthy, repetitive series of fast, sweet whistles and chirps delivered with a waltzing, metronomic quality.

Dark gray upperparts and throat, white neck and underparts. Bright red head, yellow bill. Juvenile with orange-brown head.

Saffron Finch

Sicalis flaveola

L 7" | **WS** 9-10"

INTRODUCED

A native of South America, this bright yellow finch was introduced to Oʻahu and Hawaiʻi Island in the 1960s and is now common there. Smaller, localized populations on Kauaʻi and Maui are probably the result of local releases, rather than natural dispersal. The Saffron Finch prefers dry forests and grassy coastal areas but is also present in urban locations. Aggressive during the breeding season, males will attack intruders vigorously, sometimes fighting to the death. At other times of the year, the birds form large flocks. Their song consists of high-pitched notes, interspersed with pauses.

Male bright yellow with bright orange forehead. Female (inset) pale gray with yellow breast, neck, wings, and undertail feathers.

Acknowledgments

This book would not have been possible without the support of the wonderful community of birders across the Hawaiian Islands. Countless people are working tirelessly to protect the birds we love so much, often under difficult political circumstances and certainly in some of the most challenging terrain in the world—we appreciate all that you do!

Special thanks go to Justin Hite, Stephen Rossiter, Jen Rothe, Eric VanderWerf, and Alex Wang for helpful reviews of the manuscript and to Kumu Sabra Kauka and Sam 'Ohu Gon III for their collaboration and tireless work highlighting the importance of birds to Hawaiian culture. Thanks also to the teams at Kaua'i Forest Bird Recovery Project and Kauai Endangered Seabird Recovery Project for fieldtrips that gave a deeper insight into the world of Hawai'i's rarest birds. We are grateful to Ted Floyd for proposing the idea and to George Scott for his humor and support during the writing and editing process. An extra shaka goes to Callum and Maya Raine for their patience while this book was being written.

The photographs are hugely important for this book, and we are grateful to the very talented Jack Jeffrey, Brian E. Small, David Pereksta, Robby Kohley, Jacob Drucker, Mike Danzenbaker, Arthur Morris, Annie Douglas, Dave Irons, Eric VanderWerf, I. Hutton, Jacob Spendelow, John Puschock, and Robin Baird.

Scott & Nix Acknowledgments

Many thanks to Jeffrey A. and Liz Gordon, Ted Floyd, and everyone at the American Birding Association for their good work. Thanks to Alan Poole, Miyoko Chu, and especially Kevin J. McGowan at the Cornell Lab of Ornithology for their bird measurement data sets. We give special thanks to Jack Jeffrey, Brian E. Small, and all the other contributors for their extraordinary photographs in the guide. We thank Chuck Hagner for his work on the manuscript; Paul Pianin for helping with layout and proofing the galleys; James Montalbano of Terminal Design for his typefaces; Charles Nix for the series design; and René Nedelkoff and Nancy Heinonen of Four Colour Print Group for help in shepherding this book through print production.

Image Credits

(T) = Top, (B) = Bottom, (L) = Left, (R) = Right; pages with multiple images from one source are indicated by a single credit.

XIII Jack Jeffrey. XIX Jack Jeffrey. XV André Raine. XVI Jack Jeffrey. XVII André Raine. XVIII Robby Kohley. XXII–XXIII Jack Jeffrey. XXIV Robby Kohley. XXV Jack Jeffrey. XXVII Jack Jeffrey. XXVIII Robby Kohley. XXIX André Raine. XXX David Pereksta. XXXI Jack Jeffrey. 2 Brian E. Small. 3 Jack Jeffrey. 4 Jack Jeffrey. 5 Jack Jeffrey (T). André Raine (B). 6–7 Brian E. Small. 8 A. Morris (T). Brian E. Small (B). 9 Brian E. Small. 10 Robby Kohley. 11 Brian E. Small (T), Dave Irons (B). 12 Jack Jeffrey. 13 David Pereksta (T), Jack Jeffrey (B). 14–18 Brian E. Small. 19–22 Jack Jeffrey. 23 David Pereksta. 24 Jack Jeffrey. 25 Jack Jeffrey (T), Brian E. Small (B). 26 Brian E. Small. 27 Brian E. Small. 28 Jack Jeffrey. 29 Jack Jeffrey. 30 Jack Jeffrey. 31 Jack Jeffrey. 32 John Puschock. 33–36 Jack Jeffrey. 37 David Pereksta (T), Jack Jeffrey (B). 38–39 Brian E. Small. 40 André Raine. 41 André Raine (T), Jacob Drucker (B). 42–44 Jack Jeffrey. 45 David Pereksta. 46 Brian E. Small. 47–48 Jack Jeffrey. 49 Brian E. Small. 50 Jack Jeffrey. 51 Jack Jeffrey. 52 David Pereksta. 53 David Pereksta. 54 Jack Jeffrey. 55 Jacob Spendelow. 56–57 David Pereksta. 58 André Raine. 59 Jack Jeffrey. 60–61 Robby Kohley. 62 I. Hutton. 63 Jack Jeffrey. 64 Brian E. Small. 65 Jacob Drucker. 66 Jacob Drucker. 67–69 André Raine. 70 Jack Jeffrey. 71 Jacob Drucker. 72 Robin Baird. 73 Jacob Drucker (T), André Raine (B). 74 Robby Kohley. 75 Annie Douglas 76 André Raine. 77 David Pereksta. 78 André Raine. 79 David Pereksta. 80 Robby Kohley. 81 Jacob Drucker (T), André Raine (B). 82 Mike Danzenbaker. 83 Jacob Drucker. 84 David Pereksta. 85 André Raine. 86 Mike Danzenbaker. 87 Jack Jeffrey. 88–89 André Raine. 90–98 Jack Jeffrey. 99 Brian E. Small. 100–103 Jack Jeffrey. 104 Eric VanderWerf. 105–110 Jack Jeffrey. 111 Kaeng Krachan. 112–113 Jack Jeffrey. 114 Robby Kohley. 115–117 Jack Jeffrey. 118–127 Jack Jeffrey. 128 Brian E. Small. 129–131 Jack Jeffrey. 132–133 Robby Kohley. 134 Jack Jeffrey. 135 Jack Jeffrey (T), Jacob Drucker (B). 136 Jack Jeffrey. 137 Robby Kohley (T), Jack Jeffrey (B). 138–141 Jack Jeffrey. 142 Jacob Drucker. 143–152 Jack Jeffrey. 153 Brian E. Small (L), Jack Jeffrey (R). 154–156 Jack Jeffrey.

Hawaiian Islands Bird Checklist

This is a version of the official bird checklist of the Hawaiian Islands, which includes 338 species as of 2017 and is maintained by the Hawaii Bird Records Committee (VanderWerf et al. 2018). The "Hawaiian Islands" are herein considered to include all islands that are part of the State of Hawaii plus Midway Atoll, which is not part of the State of Hawaii but an unincorporated territory of the United States, and all waters within 370.4 km (200 nautical miles) of the coast of the Hawaiian Islands.

The checklist includes all bird species known to have occurred naturally in the Hawaiian Islands and species introduced by humans that have established viable breeding populations in the wild for at least 15 years. It includes endemic species that have become extinct in historical times and introduced species that once had established breeding populations but are now extirpated, but it does not include species that are known only from fossils or subfossils.

Other bird species have been reported in the Hawaiian Islands but are regarded as hypothetical in occurrence because their identification was not certain, their natural occurrence was questionable, or, in the case of introduced species, the establishment of a viable breeding population was questionable. For a list of hypothetical species see Pyle and Pyle (2017). Taxonomy and order of taxa in this checklist follows that of the American Ornithological Society (AOS; formerly the American Ornithologists' Union [AOU]) Check-list (AOU 1998) and supplements through 2018 (Chesser et al. 2018).

For the full version of this checklist with review status, documentation, and instructions on reporting a review species visit: www.westernfieldornithologists. org/HBRC/Hawaiian_Islands_Bird_Checklist-Jan%202019.pdf

LITERATURE CITED

American Ornithologists' Union. 1998. Check-list of North American birds. 7th ed. American Ornithologists' Union, Washington, D.C. 829 pp.

Chesser, R. T., K. J. Burns, C. Cicero, J. L. Dunn, A. W. Kratter, I. J. Lovette, P. C. Rasmussen, J. V. Remsen, Jr., J. D. Rising, D. F. Stotz, B. M. Winger, and K. Winker. 2018. Fifty-ninth supplement to the American Ornithologist Society's *Check-list of North American Birds*. The Auk, Ornithological Advances, 135: 798-813.

Pyle, R.L., and P. Pyle. 2017. The Birds of the Hawaiian Islands: Occurrence, History, Distribution, and Status. B.P. Bishop Museum, Honolulu, HI, U.S.A. Version 2 (1 January 2017). http://hbs.bishopmuseum.org/birds/rlp-monograph

VanderWerf, E.A., R.E. David, P. Donaldson, R. May, H. D. Pratt, P. Pyle, and L. Tanino. 2018. First report of the Hawaii Bird Records Committee: records reviewed 2014-2016. Western Birds 49(1):2-23.

STATUS CODES

BE—Breeding Visitor endemic to Hawaii (occurs seasonally and breeds only in Hawaii)

BI—Breeding Visitor indigenous to Hawaii (occurs seasonally and breeds in Hawaii and elsewhere)

RE—Resident endemic to Hawaii (resident in the Hawaiian Islands and does not occur elsewhere)

RI—Resident indigenous to Hawaii (resident in Hawaii and also occurs elsewhere)

RXW—Resident endemic to Hawaii, extinct in the wild (exists only in captivity)

IR—Introduced, naturalized, non-native resident (currently established and breeding)

IX—Introduced, extirpated non-native (formerly established and bred)

VC—Common non-breeding visitor (migrates through or winters every year in large numbers)

VU—Uncommon non-breeding visitor (migrates through or winters every year in small numbers or locally)

VO—Occasional non-breeding visitor (visits or winters but not every year)

VA—Accidental visitor (vagrant with ≤5 records)

XE—Extinct (formerly endemic to the Hawaiian Islands)

E—Endangered species (listed as endangered under the U.S. Endangered Species Act)

T—Threatened species (listed as threatened under the U.S. Endangered Species Act)

ANATIDAE—Waterfowl
- [ ] Emperor Goose VA
- [ ] Snow Goose VU
- [ ] Greater White-fronted Goose VO
- [ ] Brant VU
- [ ] Cackling Goose VU
- [ ] Canada Goose VU
- [ ] Hawaiian Goose RE, E
- [ ] Tundra Swan VO
- [ ] Baikal Teal VA
- [ ] Garganey VO
- [ ] Blue-winged Teal VU, BI
- [ ] Cinnamon Teal VO
- [ ] Northern Shoveler VC
- [ ] Gadwall VO
- [ ] Falcated Duck VA
- [ ] Eurasian Wigeon VU
- [ ] American Wigeon VU
- [ ] Laysan Duck RE, E
- [ ] Hawaiian Duck RE, E
- [ ] Mallard VU
- [ ] Northern Pintail VC
- [ ] Green-winged Teal VU
- [ ] Canvasback VO
- [ ] Redhead VO
- [ ] Common Pochard VA
- [ ] Ring-necked Duck VU
- [ ] Tufted Duck VO
- [ ] Greater Scaup VU
- [ ] Lesser Scaup VC
- [ ] Harlequin Duck VA
- [ ] Surf Scoter VA
- [ ] Black Scoter VA
- [ ] Long-tailed Duck VA
- [ ] Bufflehead VU
- [ ] Common Goldeneye VA
- [ ] Hooded Merganser VO
- [ ] Common Merganser VA
- [ ] Red-breasted Merganser VO
- [ ] Ruddy Duck VA

ODONTOPHORIDAE—New World Quail
- [ ] California Quail IR
- [ ] Gambel' Quail IR

PHASIANIDAE—Partridges, Grouse, Turkeys, and Old World Quail
- [ ] Chukar IR
- [ ] Gray Francolin IR
- [ ] Black Francolin IR
- [ ] Erckel' Francolin IR
- [ ] Japanese Quail IR
- [ ] Red Junglefowl IR
- [ ] Kalij Pheasant IR
- [ ] Ring-necked Pheasant IR
- [ ] Indian Peafowl IR
- [ ] Wild Turkey IR

PODICIPEDIDAE—Grebes
- [ ] Pied-billed Grebe VO, BI
- [ ] Horned Grebe VA
- [ ] Red-necked Grebe VA
- [ ] Eared Grebe VA

PTEROCLIDIDAE—Sandgrouse
- [ ] Chestnut-bellied Sandgrouse IR

COLUMBIDAE—Pigeons and Doves
- [ ] Rock Pigeon IR
- [ ] Spotted Dove IR
- [ ] Zebra Dove IR
- [ ] Mourning Dove IR

CUCULIDAE—Cuckoos, Roadrunners, and Anis,

☐ Common Cuckoo VA

☐ Yellow-billed Cuckoo VA

CAPRIMULGIDAE—Nightjars

☐ Common Nighthawk VA

APODIDAE—Swifts

☐ Mariana Swiftlet IR, E

☐ Fork-tailed Swift VA

RALLIDAE—Rails, Gallinules, and Coots

☐ Sora VA

☐ Laysan Rail XE

☐ Hawaiian Rail XE

☐ Hawaiian Common Gallinule RI, E

☐ Hawaiian Coot RE, E

GRUIDAE—Cranes,

☐ Sandhill Crane VA

RECURVIROSTRIDAE—Stilts and Avocets,

☐ Black-winged Stilt VA

☐ Hawaiian Black-necked Stilt, RI, E

☐ American Avocet VA

CHARADRIIDAE—Plovers

☐ Black-bellied Plover VU

☐ Pacific Golden-Plover VC

☐ Lesser Sand-Plover VA

☐ Common Ringed Plover VA

☐ Semipalmated Plover VA

☐ Killdeer VO

☐ Eurasian Dotterel VA

SCOLOPACIDAE—Sandpipers

☐ Bristle-thighed Curlew VU

☐ Whimbrel VO

☐ Far Eastern Curlew VA

☐ Bar-tailed Godwit VO

☐ Black-tailed Godwit VA

☐ Hudsonian Godwit VA

☐ Marbled Godwit VA

☐ Ruddy Turnstone VC

☐ Red Knot VO, T

☐ Surfbird VA

☐ Ruff VO

☐ Sharp-tailed Sandpiper VU

☐ Stilt Sandpiper VA

☐ Curlew Sandpiper VO

☐ Long-toed Stint VA

☐ Red-necked Stint VO

☐ Sanderling VC

☐ Dunlin VO

☐ Baird' Sandpiper VO

☐ Little Stint VA

☐ Least Sandpiper VU

☐ White-rumped Sandpiper VA

☐ Buff-breasted Sandpiper VO

☐ Pectoral Sandpiper VU

☐ Semipalmated Sandpiper VO

☐ Western Sandpiper VO

☐ Short-billed Dowitcher VO

☐ Long-billed Dowitcher VU

☐ Pin-tailed Snipe VA

☐ Common Snipe VA

☐ Wilson' Snipe VU

☐ Terek Sandpiper VA

☐ Common Sandpiper VA

☐ Spotted Sandpiper VO

☐ Solitary Sandpiper VO

☐ Gray-tailed Tattler VO

☐ Wandering Tattler VC

☐ Lesser Yellowlegs VU

☐ Willet VO

- ☐ Spotted Redshank VA
- ☐ Greater Yellowlegs VO
- ☐ Marsh Sandpiper VA
- ☐ Wood Sandpiper VO
- ☐ Wilson' Phalarope VO
- ☐ Red-necked Phalarope VO
- ☐ Red Phalarope VU

LARIDAE—Gulls and Terns

- ☐ Black-legged Kittiwake VO
- ☐ Bonaparte' Gull VO
- ☐ Black-headed Gull VA
- ☐ Laughing Gull VU
- ☐ Franklin' Gull VU
- ☐ Mew Gull VA
- ☐ Ring-billed Gull VU
- ☐ Western Gull VA
- ☐ California Gull VA
- ☐ Herring Gull VO
- ☐ Lesser Black-backed Gull VA
- ☐ Slaty-backed Gull VO
- ☐ Glaucous-winged Gull VU
- ☐ Glaucous Gull VO
- ☐ Brown Noddy BI
- ☐ Black Noddy BI
- ☐ Blue-gray Noddy BI
- ☐ White Tern BI
- ☐ Sooty Tern BI
- ☐ Gray-backed Tern BI
- ☐ Bridled Tern VA
- ☐ Little Tern BI
- ☐ Least Tern BI, E
- ☐ Gull-billed Tern VA
- ☐ Caspian Tern VU
- ☐ Black Tern VO
- ☐ White-winged Tern VA
- ☐ Whiskered Tern VA
- ☐ Common Tern VU

- ☐ Arctic Tern VU
- ☐ Great Crested Tern VA
- ☐ Sandwich Tern VA
- ☐ Elegant Tern VA

STERCORARIIDAE—Skuas and Jaegers

- ☐ South Polar Skua VO
- ☐ Pomarine Jaeger VU
- ☐ Parasitic Jaeger VO
- ☐ Long-tailed Jaeger VO

ALCIDAE—Auks

- ☐ Ancient Murrelet VA
- ☐ Parakeet Auklet VO
- ☐ Rhinoceros Auklet VA
- ☐ Horned Puffin VO

PHAETHONTIDAE—Tropicbirds

- ☐ White-tailed Tropicbird BI
- ☐ Red-billed Tropicbird VO
- ☐ Red-tailed Tropicbird BI

GAVIIDAE—Loons

- ☐ Pacific Loon VA

DIOMEDEIDAE—Albatrosses

- ☐ Salvin' Albatross VA
- ☐ Laysan Albatross BI
- ☐ Black-footed Albatross BI
- ☐ Short-tailed Albatross BI, E

OCEANITIDAE—Southern Storm-Petrels

- ☐ Wilson' Storm-Petrel VA

HYDROBATIDAE—Northern Storm-Petrels

- ☐ Leach' Storm-Petrel VU
- ☐ Band-rumped Storm-Petrel BI, E
- ☐ Tristram' Storm-Petrel BI

PROCELLARIIDAE—Petrels and Shearwaters

- ☐ Northern Fulmar VO
- ☐ Kermadec Petrel VO
- ☐ Herald Petrel VO
- ☐ Murphy' Petrel VO
- ☐ Mottled Petrel VU
- ☐ Juan Fernandez Petrel VU
- ☐ Hawaiian Petrel BE, E
- ☐ White-necked Petrel VU
- ☐ Bonin Petrel BI
- ☐ Black-winged Petrel VU
- ☐ Cook' Petrel VU
- ☐ Stejneger' Petrel VO
- ☐ Tahiti Petrel VA
- ☐ Bulwer' Petrel BI
- ☐ Jouanin' Petrel VA
- ☐ Streaked Shearwater VA
- ☐ Pink-footed Shearwater VA
- ☐ Flesh-footed Shearwater VO
- ☐ Wedge-tailed Shearwater BI
- ☐ Buller' Shearwater VU
- ☐ Short-tailed Shearwater VU
- ☐ Sooty Shearwater VC
- ☐ Christmas Shearwater BI
- ☐ Newell' Shearwater BE, T
- ☐ Bryan' Shearwater VA

ARDEIDAE—Herons, Bitterns, and Allies

- ☐ American Bittern VA
- ☐ Great Blue Heron VA
- ☐ Gray Heron VA
- ☐ Great Egret VA
- ☐ Intermediate Egret VA
- ☐ Snowy Egret VA
- ☐ Little Blue Heron VA
- ☐ Cattle Egret IR, VU
- ☐ Green Heron VO
- ☐ Black-crowned Night-Heron RI

THRESKIORNITHIDAE—Ibises

- ☐ White-faced Ibis VU

FREGATIDAE—Frigatebirds

- ☐ Great Frigatebird BI
- ☐ Lesser Frigatebird BI

SULIDAE—Boobies

- ☐ Masked Booby BI
- ☐ Nazca Booby VA, BI
- ☐ Brown Booby BI
- ☐ Red-footed Booby BI

PHALACROCORACIDAE—Cormorants

- ☐ Pelagic Cormorant VA

PANDIONIDAE—Ospreys

- ☐ Osprey VU

ACCIPITRIDAE—Hawks, Kites, Eagles, and Allies

- ☐ Golden Eagle VA
- ☐ Northern Harrier VO
- ☐ Chinese Sparrowhawk VA
- ☐ Black Kite VA
- ☐ White-tailed Eagle VA
- ☐ Steller' Sea-Eagle VA
- ☐ Hawaiian Hawk RE, E
- ☐ Rough-legged Hawk VA

TYTONIDAE—Barn Owls

- ☐ Barn Owl IR

STRIGIDAE—Typical Owls

- ☐ Snowy Owl VA
- ☐ Pueo/Short-eared Owl RI, VO

ALCEDINIDAE—Kingfishers

☐ Belted Kingfisher VO

FALCONIDAE—Falcons

☐ Merlin VA

☐ Peregrine Falcon VU

PSITTACIDAE—New World Parrots

☐ Mitred Parakeet IR

☐ Red-masked Parakeet IR

☐ Red-crowned Parrot IR

PSITTACULIDAE—Old World Parrots

☐ Rose-ringed Parakeet IR

☐ Pale-headed Rosella IX

CORVIDAE—Crows, Jays, and Allies

☐ Hawaiian Crow RXW, E

☐ Common Raven VA

MONARCHIDAE—Monarch Flycatchers

☐ Kauai Elepaio RE

☐ Oahu Elepaio RE, E

☐ Hawaii Elepaio RE

ALAUDIDAE—Larks

☐ Eurasian Skylark IR, VA

HIRUNDINIDAE—Swallows

☐ Cliff Swallow VA

☐ Barn Swallow VA

PARIDAE—Chickadees and Titmice

☐ Varied Tit IX

PYCNONOTIDAE—Bulbuls

☐ Red-vented Bulbul IR

☐ Red-whiskered Bulbul IR

CETTIIDAE—Bush Warblers

☐ Japanese Bush-Warbler IR

ZOSTEROPIDAE—White-eyes

☐ Japanese White-eye IR

TIMALIIDAE—Babblers

☐ Greater Necklaced Laughingthrush IR

☐ Chinese Hwamei IR

☐ Red-billed Leiothrix IR

ACROCEPHALIDAE—Reed Warblers

☐ Millerbird RE, E

MUSCICAPIDAE—Old World Flycatchers

☐ White-rumped Shama IR

TURDIDAE—Thrushes

☐ Kamao XE, E

☐ Amaui XE

☐ Olomao XE, E

☐ Omao RE

☐ Puaiohi RE, E

☐ Eyebrowed Thrush VA

MIMIDAE—Mockingbirds and Thrashers

☐ Northern Mockingbird IR

STURNIDAE—Mynas and Starlings

☐ Common Myna IR

MOTACILLIDAE—Pipits and Wagtails

☐ Olive-backed Pipit VA

☐ Red-throated Pipit VA

☐ American Pipit VA

CALCARIIDAE—Longspurs and Buntings

☐ Snow Bunting VA

EMBERIZIDAE—Emberizids

☐ Savannah Sparrow VA

ICTERIDAE—Blackbirds and Meadowlarks

☐ Western Meadowlark IR

CARDINALIDAE—Cardinals, Saltators, and Allies

☐ Northern Cardinal IR

THRAUPIDAE –Tanagers and Allies

☐ Red-crested Cardinal IR

☐ Yellow-billed Cardinal IR

☐ Saffron Finch IR

☐ Yellow-faced Grassquit IR

MOHOIDAE—Hawaiian Honeyeaters

☐ Kauai Oo XE, E

☐ Oahu Oo XE

☐ Bishop' Oo XE

☐ Hawaii Oo XE

☐ Kioea XE

FRINGILLIDAE—Fringilline and Cardueline Finches and Allies

☐ Brambling VA

☐ Poo-uli XE, E

☐ Akikiki RE, E

☐ Oahu Alauahio XE, E

☐ Kakawahie XE, E

☐ Maui Alauahio RE

☐ Palila RE, E

☐ Laysan Finch RE, E

☐ Nihoa Finch RE, E

☐ Kona Grosbeak XE

☐ Lesser Koa-Finch XE

☐ Greater Koa-Finch XE

☐ Ula-ai-hawane XE

☐ Akohekohe RE, E

☐ Laysan Honeycreeper XE

☐ Apapane RE

☐ Iiwi RE

☐ Hawaii Mamo XE

☐ Black Mamo XE

☐ Ou XE, E

☐ Lanai Hookbill XE

☐ Maui Parrotbill RE, E

☐ Kauai Nukupuu XE, E

☐ Oahu Nukupuu XE

☐ Maui Nukupuu XE, E

☐ Akiapolaau RE, E

☐ Lesser Akialoa XE

☐ Kauai Akialoa XE, E

☐ Oahu Akialoa XE

☐ Maui-nui Akialoa XE

☐ Anianiau RE

☐ Hawaii Amakihi RE

☐ Oahu Amakihi RE

☐ Kauai Amakihi RE

☐ Greater Amakihi XE

☐ Hawaii Creeper RE, E

☐ Akekee RE, E

☐ Oahu Akepa XE

☐ Maui Akepa XE, E

☐ Hawaii Akepa RE, E

☐ House Finch IR

☐ Yellow-fronted Canary IR

☐ Common Redpoll VA

☐ Island Canary IR

PASSERIDAE—Old World Sparrows

☐ House Sparrow IR

ESTRILDIDAE –Estrildid Finches

☐ Lavender Waxbill IR

☐ Orange-cheeked Waxbill IR

☐ Common Waxbill IR

☐ Red Avadavat IR

☐ African Silverbill IR

☐ Java Sparrow IR

☐ Scaly-breasted Munia IR

☐ Chestnut Munia IR

Species Index

U

W

Y

Z

THE AMERICAN BIRDING ASSOCIATION STATE FIELD GUIDE SERIES

ARIZONA
ISBN 978-1-935622-60-4

CALIFORNIA
ISBN 978-1-935622-50-5

CAROLINAS
ISBN 978-1-935622-63-5

COLORADO
ISBN 978-1-935622-43-7

FLORIDA
ISBN 978-1-935622-48-2

HAWAI'I
ISBN 978-1-935622-71-0

ILLINOIS
ISBN 978-1-935622-62-8

MASSACHUSETTS
ISBN 978-1-935622-66-6

MICHIGAN
ISBN 978-1-935622-67-3

MINNESOTA
ISBN 978-1-935622-59-8

NEW JERSEY
ISBN 978-1-935622-42-0

NEW YORK
ISBN 978-1-935622-51-2

OHIO
ISBN 978-1-935622-70-3

OREGON
ISBN 978-1-935622-68-0

PENNSYLVANIA
ISBN 978-1-935622-52-9

TEXAS
ISBN 978-1-935622-53-6

WASHINGTON
ISBN 978-1-935622-72-7

WISCONSIN
ISBN 978-1-935622-69-7

Helen Raine is a writer and conservationist living in Kaua'i. Her passion for birds has taken her around the world undertaking fieldwork in England, Malta, Peru, Zambia, and Hawai'i. As a freelance journalist, she focuses on the environment, travel, and is the author of several wildlife guide books.

André F. Raine, Ph.D. is the project manager for an endangered seabird project on the island of Kaua'i, where he has worked since 2011. He focuses on the conservation of seabird species, as well as assisting similar projects on Lāna'i and Hawai'i Island. Originally from Bermuda, he has led conservation projects around the World including the Peruvian Amazon, the plains of Zambia, and the moorlands of England. He is the author of many scientific publications, as well as several photographic bird guides.

Jack Jeffrey is a professional bird photographer, birding guide, and wildlife biologist. A resident of the Big Island of over 45 years, he is intimately familiar with Hawai'i's remote rainforests, hidden valleys, and endemic birds. Jack is recipient of the prestigious "Ansel Adams Award for Nature Photography" and is a USFWS "Endangered Species Champion." His work can be seen at jackjeffreyphoto.com.

Quick Index

See the Species Index for a complete listing of all the birds in the *American Birding Association Field Guide to Birds of Hawai'i*.